Faces of the Berlin Wall

DIVIDED LIVES AND LEGACIES THIRTY YEARS AFTER THE FALL

Edited by:

Michael A. Di Giovine, Ph.D.
*Director, West Chester University Museum of
Anthropology and Archaeology*

Cover image by Evie Alport. © West Chester University, Museum of Anthropology and Archaeology.

Kendall Hunt
publishing company

www.kendallhunt.com
Send all inquiries to:
4050 Westmark Drive
Dubuque, IA 52004-1840

Copyright © 2022 by Kendall Hunt Publishing Company

ISBN: 978-1-7924-4016-8

All rights reserved. No part of this publication may be reproduced, stored in a retrieval system, or transmitted, in any form or by any means, electronic, mechanical, photocopying, recording, or otherwise, without the prior written permission of the copyright owner.

Published in the United States of America

In memory of our colleague and friend
Dr. Frauke I. Schnell
(1963–2020)

CONTENTS

List of Figures ix

West Chester University Museum of
Anthropology and Archaeology xv

Acknowledgments xix

Introduction   Faces of the Berlin Wall: Divided Lives and
Legacies Thirty Years After the Fall 1
Michael A. Di Giovine, Ph.D.

History of the Wall

Chapter 1   A City Divided: The History of the Berlin Wall 7
Stephen Darrell

Chapter 2   How the Berlin Wall Was Built 19
Thomas Haughey, MFA

Politics between East and West

Chapter 3   Behind Enemy Lines: America in West Berlin
1945–1989 25
Christopher DiMaria

Chapter 4   The GDR: A Surveillance State 33
Brad Nehls, Jr.

Chapter 5   The Stasi, East Germany's Powerful and Secret
Intelligence Agency 41
Mark Duffy

Chapter 6	Alfred Cardinal Bengsch: Navigating the Split City of Berlin..47 *Brenda Gaydosh*	
Chapter 7	Escaping East Berlin: The Bethke Brothers........57 *Chase Fitzgerald*	

Lived Experiences

Chapter 8	Globalization and the East-West Divide............65 *Emily Rodden and Jacqueline Wanjek*
Chapter 9	Tourism and Mobility in the Eastern Bloc..........73 *Michael A. Di Giovine, Ph.D.*
Chapter 10	Divided Germany, Divided Sports.......................91 *Jenna Walmer*
Chapter 11	Through Their Eyes..97 *Margaret Hartnett*
Chapter 12	Connections: Memoirs of an American Historian in the Communist East Bloc.............117 *Claude Foster; edited by Brenda Gaydosh*
Chapter 13	Tears in Bitterfeld...125 *Claude Foster*
Chapter 14	New Year's Eve, 1989..129 *Dana Cressler*

The Afterlife of the Berlin Wall

Chapter 15	Creating "Berlin" and Creating "the Wall".........135 *Bruno von Lutz*
Chapter 16	Commemorating the Berlin Wall.......................149 *Natalie Fenner*

Chapter 17	The Commercialization of the Berlin Wall .... 159 *Foster W. Krupp and Christian Sabree*
Chapter 18	The Berlin Wall in Popular Culture .... 169 *Brianna A. Eldridge*
Chapter 19	Concerts at the Berlin Wall .... 177 *Jim McAllister*
Chapter 20	The Persistence of Division .... 183 *Brittany Siemon*

Afterword

Chapter 21	Commentary: Walls Divide .... 189 *Emily Rodden*
Chapter 22	Witnesses of Stone: Monuments of the Socialist Past in Bulgaria .... 193 *Nikolai Vukov, Ph.D.*

The Exhibition

Chapter 23	Making the Exhibition .... 203 *Michael A. Di Giovine, Ph.D.*
Chapter 24	Interactive Exhibits in *Faces of the* *Berlin Wall* .... 211 *Marshall Goodman and Aiden Max*
Chapter 25	The Art of the West Berlin Wall .... 219 *Anissa Kunchick*
Chapter 26	Leaving Our Mark .... 225 *Michael A. Di Giovine, Ph.D.*

LIST OF FIGURES

Fig. 0.1	The Museum of Anthropology and Archaeology, with the Berlin Wall model in front	xvi
Fig. I.1	Student co-curators celebrating the exhibition opening	3
Fig. 1.1	The History of the Berlin Wall exhibit	7
Fig. 1.2	Berlin: Allied Occupation Zones	8
Fig. 1.3	Berlin Airlift medal	9
Fig. 1.4	East and West German currency	9
Fig. 1.5	Immigration to West Germany (W. German Data)	10
Fig. 1.6	Rubik's Cube, c. 1980	13
Fig. 1.7	Postcard commemorating November 10 celebrations	14
Fig. 1.8	Timeline of the Berlin Wall	17
Fig. 2.1	Berlin Wall schematics	20
Fig. 2.2	Students Examining the Cantilevered Section of the Berlin Wall at the German Society of Philadelphia	21
Fig. 3.1	U.S. Intelligence exhibit	27
Fig. 3.2	EAI PACE TR-10	28
Fig. 3.3	Piece of the Berlin Wall collected by then-Lt. Dana Cressler	29
Fig. 3.4	Frank Trolio, WWII veteran stationed in Berlin in 1945, visits *Faces of the Berlin Wall* with museum director Michael A. Di Giovine	30
Fig. 4.1	Stasi exhibit	36
Fig. 4.2	AK-47 and M-16 on display	38
Fig. 4.3	Stasi uniform on display	39
Fig. 6.1	Alfred Cardinal Bengsch	47
Fig. 6.2	Pages from Cardinal Bengsch's Stasi file	52
Fig. 7.1	WCU's memorial to those fallen trying to escape East Berlin	59

Fig. 8.1	Western and West German products	66
Fig. 8.2	Soviet and East German products	68
Fig. 8.3	Sandmann doll (East Germany) and Barbie doll (West Germany)	69
Fig. 9.1	Tourism and Mobility in the East	74
Fig. 9.2	*Postcard Vacations* exhibit	74
Fig. 9.3	Postcard booklet from Tallinn, the capital of Estonia, which was part of the USSR at the time	78
Fig. 9.4	Postcard from Sigulda, Latvia (part of the USSR) featuring a monument to Lenin	79
Fig. 9.5	Tourist souvenir of a socialist monument	79
Fig. 9.6	Postcard of a tourist hostel in Ribaritsa, Bulgaria	80
Fig. 9.7	Souvenir spoon from Lake Balatan, Hungary, a popular destination for East German tourists	81
Fig. 9.8	Moscow 1980 Olympics postcards	82
Fig. 9.9	Soviet guidebook to East Berlin	83
Fig. 9.10	Soviet postcard of the Brandenburg Gate, Berlin	84
Fig. 9.11	Postcard showing the good life at the Bulgarian seaside resort of Primorsko, site of an international youth camp	85
Fig. 10.1	Uli Meunch's Olympic cycling jersey	94
Fig. 10.2	Sports medals from the GDR	95
Fig. 11.1	Memorabilia from Uli's East German childhood	100
Fig. 11.2	Inka and Apollo cigarettes	101
Fig. 11.3	Five generations of Nitsche/Finnin women: Ivonne Finnin and family	104
Fig. 11.4	Ivonne's East German immunization records and favorite book	106
Fig. 11.5	Pioneer uniforms	107
Fig. 11.6	Barbara Springer	109
Fig. 11.7	Barbara Springer's *Gesselenbrief*	110
Fig. 11.8	Returning for a piece of the wall	112
Fig. 11.9	Artifacts reminiscent of Kordula's youth in West Germany	114

Fig. 12.1	Claude Foster	117
Fig. 14.1	Second Lt. Dana Cressler and wife in front of the Brandenburg Gate, East Berlin	130
Fig. 14.2	Chipping a piece of the wall, December 1989	131
Fig. 14.3	New Year's Eve at the wall	131
Fig. 14.4	New Year's Eve at the wall	131
Fig. 14.5	Scaling the wall	132
Fig. 14.6	Dana Cressler and wife on the wall	132
Fig. 15.1	Student co-curators visiting the Berlin Wall at Philadelphia's German Society with its director Anton "Tony" Michels	136
Fig. 15.2	*Mauerspringer* ("Wall Jumper")	139
Fig. 15.3	Pin from German-American Institute	142
Fig. 15.4	The reconstructed Berlin castle with the city's iconic TV tower in the background	145
Fig. 15.5	The author delivering this public lecture at West Chester University on September 19, 2019	146
Fig. 16.1	Various forms of commemoration: postcards; stamps; t-shirts; cherry blossoms	151
Fig. 16.2	Postcard showing the Soviet-led destruction of the Church of Reconciliation	153
Fig. 16.3	Chapel of Reconciliation	154
Fig. 16.4	Mauer Weg in springtime	154
Fig. 16.5	Cherry blossoms and balloons represented in the exhibit	155
Fig. 16.6	*Lichtgrenze 2014*	156
Fig. 17.1	Commercialization of the Berlin Wall exhibit	161
Fig. 17.2	Pieces of the wall sold to tourists	162
Fig. 17.3	Chipping pieces off the wall in 1990	163
Fig. 17.4	Pieces of the Berlin Wall collected by WCU professors	164
Fig. 17.5	Homeopathic remedy, apparently made from pulverized pieces of the wall	165
Fig. 17.6	LEGO Berlin set	166
Fig. 18.1	The Berlin Wall in Popular Culture exhibit	170

Fig. 19.1	Listening to David Hasselhoff on New Year's Eve at the wall	180
Fig. 20.1	The Persistence of Division exhibit	183
Fig. 20.2	"Berlin at Night," photographed by Canadian astronaut and International Space Station Commander Chris Hadfield	184
Fig. 22.1	*Witnesses of Stone* exhibition in the Francis Harvey Green Library	194
Fig. 22.2	Monument to Lenin in the village of Pet Mogili, Shumen area	196
Fig. 22.3	Monument to the Soviet army in the town of Russe	196
Fig. 22.4	Sculptural composition at the base of the "Brotherly Mound to the Fallen in the Antifascist Struggle," Sofia	196
Fig. 22.5	Monument to fallen antifascists in the village of Hrabrino, Plovdiv area	196
Fig. 22.6	Sculptural decoration representing youth labor and a happy life under communism	197
Fig. 22.7	Interior decoration of the house-monument to the Bulgarian Communist Party on Buzludja Peak	198
Fig. 22.8	Monument to the first tractor during the postwar mechanization of agriculture, village of Izvorovo, Haskovo area	198
Fig. 23.1	Uli Muensch talking with students about his defection from East Germany	204
Fig. 23.2	Constructing the wall	205
Fig. 23.3	Delivering the concrete wall, which would become our memorial to fallen victims	205
Fig. 23.4	Cataloging artifacts from Eastern Europe	206
Fig. 23.5	8th and 9th graders from Unionville High School tour the exhibition with co-curators Christian Sabree (left) and Aaron Gallant (right)	207
Fig. 23.6	Deconstructing the wall	208

Fig. 24.1	Tablet home page	212
Fig. 24.2	WCU students in the ELS program leave their mark on the wall	213
Fig. 24.3	Students from Windsor Academy creatively find blank space to graffiti the wall	214
Fig. 24.4	Anissa Kunchick painting the memorial to fallen victims	215
Fig. 24.5	Ivonne Finnin examining the memorial	216
Fig. 25.1	Images from Berlin Wall graffiti that provided inspiration for our interpretation.	220
Fig. 25.2	Graffiti of a mysterious face on the German Society of Philadelphia's Berlin Wall segment	221
Fig. 25.3	Student co-curator Christian Sabree enjoys a minute of calm before the opening reception	221
Fig. 25.4	Side view of Bauhaus benches and west side of the wall	222
Fig. 26.1	Letter from an 8th-grade student	226
Fig. 26.2	Students graffitiing the wall	227
Fig. 26.3	Samples of visitors' graffiti	228

West Chester University Museum of Anthropology and Archaeology

The West Chester University Museum of Anthropology and Archaeology is a dynamic teaching museum in which students co-curate insightful exhibits based on the Department of Anthropology and Sociology's historical, artistic, primatological, archaeological and ethnographic collections. Our collections span the globe and range from the prehistoric to modern, with a particular focus on the Americas (Native North and Central America, U.S.-Mexico borderlands, contemporary Latin America), East Africa, and Europe. Located in the historic Old Library building, at the heart of West Chester University's main campus, the museum is a vibrant space that is welcomes the campus community and to the public.

Our mission is to serve as a welcoming, vibrant center where faculty, students, and the public can connect and experience new ideas through our focus on teaching, research, collecting and public engagement. The Museum aspires to further the University's Plan for Excellence by serving as a leader in community engagement and enhancing the quality of life for all campus community members. It is an inspiring classroom and promotes a collaborative culture of thought and inquiry by connecting academic units across the West Chester campus together with a larger public audience.

Originally founded in 2007 as the Old Library Atrium Museum, the Museum of Anthropology and Archaeology is West Chester University's sole teaching laboratory for museum studies. In it, students learn the ins and outs of exhibit development and curation, museum administration, collections management, and audience

Fig. 0.1: The Museum of Anthropology and Archaeology, with the Berlin Wall model in front

research. The Museum maintains a permanent collection of archaeological and ethnographic materials that form the core of the museum's exhibits; however, loans of historical, artistic, and cultural items also greatly enhance the content of the themed exhibitions.

The Department of Anthropology and Sociology houses the Museum, which is under the direction of Dr. Michael A. Di Giovine. The anthropology program's array of museum studies, archaeology, heritage, and tourism courses provides a solid theoretical foundation on the role that objects and exhibitions play in developing interpretive narratives for public education and outreach. The Museum of Anthropology and Archaeology acts as a teaching facility in which students gain valuable hands-on experience curating an exhibit from start to finish—from brainstorming exhibition topics to planning the exhibit, from installation of artifacts to the production of a museum catalog. Past exhibits have utilized the department's rich archaeological and ethnographic collections spanning diverse time periods, as well as private collections, and frequently involves collaboration with faculty experts across disciplines and departments at West Chester University. They have addressed topics such as Native American culture, The Silk Road, foodways, enculturation through children's toys, and human rights. Faculty across disciplines are encouraged to utilize these exhibits in their classroom instruction. The WCU Museum of Anthropology and Archaeology is officially part of the West Chester University Museums and Special Archives (WCUMSA), which is composed of our institution, the Francis Harvey Green Library, and the WCU Special Collections. The WCUMSA is a member of the American Alliance of Museums.

Past Exhibits

2007	The Lenape Gamwing Ceremony: A Window into the Delaware Big House Rite
2008	History Recycled: The Journey of the Blue Ball (Tavern)
2009	Archaeology of Early Quakers in Southeastern Pennsylvania: The Robert Pyle Site
2010	Indigenous Andean Hats and Headdresses: The Edmundo Morales Collection
2011	Material Culture of the American Indian: The Carlton Thomas Collection
2012	Bridging Asia: Trade and Culture in the Indian Ocean
2014	Enculturation: Learning Our Cultural Identity as Children
2016	Feasting and Foodways: Creating Community through Time in the Southeastern Delaware Valley
2017	The Struggle for Human Rights in Latin America, 1967–2017
2018	*Rwanda Nziza:* Beautiful Rwanda
2019	Faces of the Berlin Wall: Divided Lives and Legacies 30 Years After the Fall
2020	Earth Day at 50: Lessons for a Sustainable Future (*opened 2021 due to COVID-19*)
2021	WCU 150: History and Heritage

Special Events Associated with *Faces of the Berlin Wall*

"Witnesses of Stone" public lecture by Dr. Nikolai Vukov, Museum of Ethnology, Sofia, Bulgaria, April 25, 2019.

Opening Reception, April 26, 2019.

Witnesses of Stone: Monuments of the Socialist Past in Bulgaria Temporary Exhibition, guest curated by Dr. Nikolai Vukov, April 26–June 1, 2019.

Postcard Vacations: The Many Faces of Travel and Leisure Behind the Berlin Wall temporary exhibition, guest curated by Rossitza Ohridska-Olson, May 9–September 27, 2019.

Ethnic Studies Reception, May 3, 2019.

"The Berlin Wall and 'The Berlin Wall'" public lecture by Dr. Bruno von Lutz, German-American Institute, Saarland, Germany, September 19, 2019.

Closing Reception and tearing down the wall, March 5, 2020.

ACKNOWLEDGMENTS

This exhibition could not have been mounted without diverse skills of our student co-curators, as well as the exceptionally generous donations of time, artifacts, equipment, and funds from the following people:

Curator
Michael A. Di Giovine, Ph.D.
Associate Professor of Anthropology
Director, Museum of Anthropology and Archaeology
West Chester University of Pennsylvania

Designer
Tom Haughey, MFA
Assistant Professor of Technical Direction and Sound Design
Department of Theater and Dance
West Chester University of Pennsylvania

Curatorial Consultant
Rossitza Ohridska-Olson, Ph.D.
Director, Vizantia, Inc.
Sofia, Bulgaria

Student co-curators
Stephen Darrell
Christopher DiMaria
Shahd El Gerzawy
Brianna Eldridge
Natalie Fenner
Aaron Gallant
Margaret Hartnett
Foster W. Krupp
Anissa Kunchick
Aiden Max

Brad Nehls, Jr.
Emily Rodden
Christian Sabree
Brittany Siemon
Jacqueline Wanjek

Oral Histories
Ivonne Finnin
Uli Muench
Kordula Segler-Stahl
Estate of Barbara Raichel Springer

From West Chester University
Radha Pyati, Dean, College of the Sciences and Mathematics
Joseph Santivasci, Associate Vice President for Campus Planning and Outreach
Heather Wholey, Professor and Chair, Department of Anthropology and Sociology
Tom Clark, Associate Director of Facilities
Jenna Birch & Brigid Gallagher, WCU Alumni Association
Mary Page, Director, Francis Harvey Green Library
Walter Cressler, Reference Librarian, F. H. Green Library
Amanda Brooks, Library Technician, F. H. Green Library IMC
Robert McGuckin, Manager, Graphics and Printing
Ainsley Hume & Jennifer O'Leary, F. H. Green Library
Frauke I. Schnell, Professor and Chair, Department of Political Science
Marwan Kreidie, Department of Political Science
Peter Loedel, Assistant Vice President for International Programs
Brenda Gaydosh, Associate Professor, Department of History
Michael Pearson, Associate Professor, Department of Communications and Media
Lisa Kirschenbaum & Jannekin Smucker, Department of History
David Bolton, Associate Professor, Department of Education
John Leveille, Associate Professor, Department of Anthropology and Sociology

Jordan Schugar, Department of English
Karen Watkins, Department of Art + Design
Kristin Williams, Information Services and Technology
Nancy Gainer, Assistant Vice President for Communications and Marketing
Nick Pascarosa, Scene Shop Coordinator
Matt Born, Graphics and Printing
Laura Pyott, Department of Mathematics
Marcia Berger

From Near and Far
Nikolai Vukov, Museum of Ethnology, Bulgarian Academy of Sciences, Sofia, Bulgaria
Bruno von Lutz, Director, German-American Institute, Saarland, Germany
Anton "Tony" Michels, Director, German Society of Philadelphia
The Computer Church
Chester County Historical Society
Col. Lewis Cressler
Col. Dana Cressler
John and Ivonne Finnin
Uli Muench
Kordula Segler-Stahl
Keith Bayliss
Jennifer and Jody Springer
Joan Hartnett
The Foster Family
Laura, Alex and Sebastian Di Giovine
Evie Allport
Stefani Demoss and Matt Blue, Kendall-Hunt Publishers

INTRODUCTION

Faces of the Berlin Wall: Divided Lives and Legacies Thirty Years After the Fall

Michael A. Di Giovine, Ph.D.

One wall. Two sides. A city—a people—divided.

Erected in 1961 by the Soviet-aligned East Germany to stop the flow of migrants to the west, the Berlin Wall stretched for nearly 100 miles. Though it fully encircled the U.S.-allied West Berlin, it ironically constrained the mobility of its own inhabitants in the East. But the wall was not simply a structure in concrete and steel. It was a demarcation of borders between communism and capitalism, East and West. It projected power and security for the Eastern bloc. It symbolized oppression for the West, of the Cold War division of the world at the time. It was an apparatus of state power, a means of surveillance and control. It was also a canvas for expression, of ideological messaging artfully painted upon its stoic form. It was a sign of (im)mobility, representing the impossibility of passage for some, and the gift of free movement for others.

When the Berlin Wall fell 30 years ago, it was hailed as the fall of the Iron Curtain, a victory for the West. But the wall lives on as a monument to the fallen, a destination to visitors, souvenirs to tourists, and a symbol of loss to the nostalgic. The wall was not simply a construction, but a culmination of lived experiences that has had a significant cultural impact on Germans and the global community, and continues to be relevant 30 years later.

This immersive exhibition engages visitors to move between sectors, between realities, between and beyond the ideological divisions of east and west, socialism and capitalism, mobility and immobility. Entering the space, visitors find themselves at a checkpoint divided by a 10-foot-long, 12-foot-high representation of the Berlin Wall; they are told to enjoy their own freedom to choose which way to go—something so often taken for granted in Germany and the United States 30 years after the Fall. Mirror-image tableaux greet the visitors. Turning left, visitors would enter the U.S. sector of West Germany. Turning right, they would enter the Soviet sector of East Germany. Either way, visitors will pass through the respective government's surveillance mechanism.

Moving to the right, toward the East, visitors are confronted with starkly plain and simple colors, whitewashed and neutral. A Stasi soldier standing at a desk scattered with copies of actual files on a West Chester professor and a Catholic priest loom ominously. A sense of muted immobility penetrates the space; a vast timeline, punctuated with real artifacts from the era, stretches across the room. Yet visitors are reminded that, despite the constraints of living in the East, life goes on, people still move. An engaging exhibit on tourism in the Eastern bloc—filled with real artifacts from the era, including a suitcase full of clothing, a camera, maps and guidebooks, postcards, souvenirs, and a passport—complicate the well-known narrative of immobility and provide insight into the ways in which unity among citizens behind the Iron Curtain fostered a sense of unity through leisure. Visitors can also examine artifacts from daily life in the 1970s and 1980s—from soaps and coffee makers to fashion magazines and movie posters, to toys and other leisure goods.

Toward the left, to the West, visitors are met by a U.S. official, standing next to a desk with an analog computer used to crack Soviet codes, and a briefcase used a CIA officer in 1970s Europe. Yet the aesthetic differences between East and West are immediately stark: the drab of the East gives way to shocking vibrancy as visitors are overwhelmed by the color and energy of the graffitied wall in the West. While visitors to the East reluctantly approach the timeline—looking but not touching—in the West they are free to touch it, and even to scribble their own graffiti on one portion. The contrasts continue. Although in the East the everyday materials may seem exotic and dated to some, on the West side, daily artifacts seem almost ironically banal: jeans, Marlborough cigarettes, Nivea lotion, even bananas. The banality gives viewers pause to consider that which we may take for granted in the West, yet are tantalizingly seductive, desired, and exotic to those who are embargoed from global markets.

This experience of East and West culminates in a unified exhibit on the other side of the wall, where visitors see these narratives through the eyes of four Germans who have connections with our own community—each with a different story, a different perspective, a different recollection of the time: One West German lived meters away from the wall and experienced life under Western occupation, the other married a solider and left for Britain, only to be drawn back to Berlin when she heard the news of the wall's demise. One East German was a prominent youth athlete for the socialist republic, yet secretly harbored a desire to defect which

Fig. I.1: Student co-curators celebrating the exhibition opening. *Front row:* Aiden Max, Jacqueline Wanjek, Dr. Michael A. Di Giovine, Marshall Goodman, Brianna Eldridge, Brittany Siemon. *Back row:* Christopher DiMaria, Brad Nehls, Jr., Anissa Kunchick, Natalie Fenner, Margaret Hartnett, Christian Sabree, Emily Rodden, Foster W. Krupp, Aaron Gallant. [Not pictured: Stephen Darrell, Shahd El Gerzawy]

almost cost him his life; the other lived an idyllic childhood supported by the socialist government. Life is complex, and these oral histories—coupled with the narrators' personal effects—once again show how the wall divided not only lives, but perspectives, mentalities.

As visitors make their way out of Berlin, into the next room, they experience the afterlife of the wall—its commemoration, memorialization, touristification, and commoditization. While Berliners today memorialize the wall in a variety of ways—from stamps and postcards to tourist itineraries—this room shows just how global, just how iconic, the wall and its famous moment of demise was. Japanese cherry blossoms and U.S. stamps reveal international links with Berlin; Broadway shows, children's books, and rock albums from Anglo-American groups emphasize just how deeply the wall permeates pop culture in our own society. And postcards upon postcards reveal not only a need to see, to experience, to commemorate, but also to commercialize the wall. Capitalism is in full swing as visitors gaze at "fake" pieces of the wall, tourist souvenirs, a LEGO set, and even homeopathic medicine supposedly made of pulverized pieces of the wall. Standing in place for nearly as long as it has been down, we can understand how the iconic Berlin Wall impacted, and continues to impact, the lives of those in Germany and throughout the world.

History of the Wall

Chapter 1: **A City Divided: The History of the Berlin Wall**
Stephen Darrell

Chapter 2: **How the Berlin Wall Was Built**
Thomas Haughey, MFA

CHAPTER 1

A City Divided: The History of the Berlin Wall

Stephen Darrell

Fig. 1.1: The History of the Berlin Wall Exhibit

The Wall that divided Berlin was a physical manifestation of the cultural and ideological divide that characterized Germany and the world during the Cold War years (1945–1990). From the partition of Germany and Berlin into Allied Occupation zones after

Contributed by Stephen Darrel. © Kendall Hunt Publishing Company

World War II to German Reunification in 1990, Germany was the battleground between capitalism and socialism. The history of Berlin and the Berlin Wall is a microcosm of Germany itself.

After Germany's surrender that ended World War II, the Allied Powers divided German into Occupation zones to administer and rebuilt the nation. The four zones were controlled by the American, British, French, and Soviet militaries. As the capital, Berlin was also divided into the zones even though it was located squarely in Soviet territory (See Figure 1.2). This partition was the beginning of the ideological divide; three of the zones were administered by capitalist governments while the Soviet zone was a socialist government. The ideological differences prevented German from creating a new united government in Berlin, an island of Western influence 110 miles inside the Soviet zone.

Fig. 1.2: Berlin: Allied Occupation Zones

In 1947 the French, British and American zones were united into one. This area became known as West Germany and was opposed by the Soviets that controlled the area that became known as East Germany, and within which the traditional German capital of Berlin lay. By 1948 the problem became a crisis, as the Soviets desired complete control over Berlin, if they could not control all of Germany. Known as the Berlin Crisis of 1948, the Soviet authorities closed all land routes to Berlin from West Germany. Rather than capitulate to the pressure, the Allies began the Berlin Airlift. From June 1948 to May 1949 the people of West Berlin were supplied their basic necessities via air (U.S. Department of State, 2019a). Numerous forgotten U.S. service members were honored with the Medal for Human Action (U.S. National Archives 2019),[1] commonly called the Berlin Airlift Medal, for their participation in the operation. More than just American forces contributed; crews from the United States, Canada, Australia, South Africa, Great Britain, and France flew more than 200,000 sorties each year, delivering 12,941 tons of food, fuel, and supplies each day. This performance of unity and determination among Western countries demonstrated the strength of the Western alliance, and the Soviet Union did not attack for fear of escalating the crisis. Yet it also hastened the solidification of two separate German states and the construction of the Berlin Wall.

Fig. 1.3: Berlin Air Lift Medal

Fig. 1.4: East and West German currency

---

[1] The official name for this award is listed as Medal of Humane Action, however in the regulation it is referred to as the Medal for Humane Action.

Indeed, there were other events in the same period that led to the division of the German state. For example, prior to the closing of the interzone border was the introduction of currency reform. In June 1948 both West and East Germany occupation authorities began issuing new currency. The Deutschmark replaced the Reichsmark as the national currency in the West, while the Soviet issued Deutschmark, referred to as the East Mark (*Ost Mark*) was the currency of the East (Richie, 1998, pp. 659–660; U.S. Dept. of State, 2019a). By the next year, Germany had officially become two sovereign states; the Federal Republic of Germany (FRG) was officially announced on May 23, 1949; and the German Democratic Republic (GDR) was created shortly thereafter, on October 7 (Richie, 1998,pp. 674–675). The FRG followed the capitalistic Western model; the GDR followed the socialist Soviet model. The currency issued throughout the Cold War reflected the ideologies of each Germany. FRG currency used traditional symbols like the eagle, while GDR currency used socialist symbols such as grain. By the end of their existence, the GDR had also added German proletariat heroes. The five-mark banknote issued in 1975 featured the portrait of Thomas Müntzer, a leader of the German Peasants' War (1525) (Anon, 2019; Scott 1989). The countries issued different stamps and, more importantly, different passports, as well.

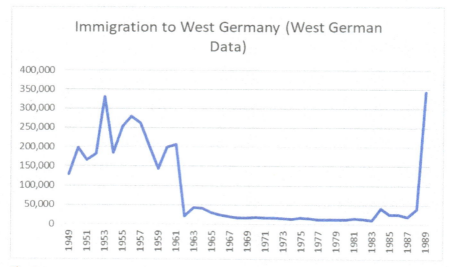

Fig. 1.5: Immigration to West Germany (W. German Data).
Source: The author, based on Judt 1997.

Living in a divided city offered challenges to Berliners. People who were born and grew up as German now were divided into West and East Berliners. Travelling within the city could even require a passport, and as time went on movement became more difficult, particularly for citizens of the GDR, who would move across the border disproportionately for work and even to live. Immigration data (see Fig. 1.3) shows that, and as time went on movement became more difficult, particularly for citizens of the GDR, who would move across the border disproportionately for work and even to live. Immigration data (see Figure 1.5) shows that throughout the 1950s people flowed from the GDR to the FRG by over a hundred thousand a year, largely unencumbered by border controls (Judt, 1997). This immigration from the East was unsustainable for the GDR. As Deane and David Heller pointed out in 1962, most of the people fleeing across the border to West Berlin were from the educated class—doctors and scientists (Heller & Heller 1962, p. 232). Once in West Berlin, they were considered citizens of West Germany and were issued a West German passport. A nation, particularly one with socialized education, cannot afford to continuously lose the specialists that they paid to educate only to have them benefit another nation. Because of the need to stem this loss of citizens, in 1958 Soviet Premier Khrushchev demanded the withdrawal of foreign troops from West Berlin. The subsequent Berlin Crisis (1958–61) originally called for the withdrawal to be completed in six months. Fear was high that the argument over Berlin would lead to World War III, or a need to revive the Berlin Airlift (Heller & Heller 1962, p. 12–15; U.S. Department of State, 2019b). In 1959, journalist Joseph Fleming wrote a story for United Press International (UPI) that was to include a map showing the air routes from the FRG to West Berlin should the crisis escalate once again; our collection includes an original mailing of the map from UPI. Fortunately, for Berliners and the world, such extreme measures were never necessary.

Khrushchev's eventual solution was simpler than war. In August 1961 construction of a hard border separating East and West Berlin started. What the world now knows as the Berlin Wall—96 miles of concrete slabs 12 feet high, 65 miles of fencing, and the "death strip" of landmines and armed surveillance—did not happen overnight (Klein, 2019). The beginning of the Wall was much humbler. Originally, the wall was nothing more than a barbed wire fence marking the border. Such a barrier, even guarded, was little trouble for many East Berliners to overcome. They simply jumped the wire to freedom in the West (Heller & Heller, 1962, pp. 32–35). One of those that decided to defect was Conrad Schumann, whose leap was captured by a photographer and memorialized as a symbol of resistance to the Wall; his story was published in the *Life* magazine on display. Though he was among the first wave of escapees, he was not the last. Daniel Schorr was one of the many journalists in Berlin covering the Wall and the refugees crossing it. Those that made it across or died trying are honored in our memory as heroes for freedom. Those that did not attempt the crossing are often forgotten, despite their victimization; for example, poignant photographs on display in our exhibit reveal the divided lives of children at the wall.

With its emphasis on restricting mobility, the Wall seemed to be turning the GDR into a prison for its people. For Western politicians, the wall came to symbolize the social control and lack of freedom that defined the Soviet Union against the democratic, capitalistic system in the West. President John F. Kennedy visited Berlin and the Wall in 1963, giving his famous "Ich bin ein Berliner" ("I am a Berliner") speech. In that speech he stated that "freedom has many difficulties and democracy is not perfect, but we have never had to put a wall up to keep our people in, to prevent them from leaving us . . . the wall is the most obvious and vivid demonstration of the failures of the Communist system" (ISN, 2019). The speech may have been written before arriving in Germany, but President Kennedy's visit to Checkpoint Charlie prior to delivering it may have shown him the truth in his words.

By the 1980s this prison wall started to crack. Although the wall certainly served to stamp out the kind of mass exodus from East to West that occurred before the Wall's construction (see Fig. 1.3 again), and the severity of its militarization—which led to many deaths in the early years—seemed also to have staved off attempts, people nevertheless continued to escape over, under, or through the Wall through the 70s and 80s. As other Socialist countries started to look to the West for economic opportunities, the fall of the wall became inevitable. Goods, for example, began to trickle out of the Soviet bloc. In 1980 a Hungarian inventor, Ernõ Rubik, licensed his "Magic Cube" to Ideal Toy Company for worldwide distribution as Rubik's Cube (National Museum of Play,

2019; Rubik's Brand Ltd., 2019). For anyone who was over 5 years old during this decade, the Rubik's Cube was a huge fad around the world; its popularity would reveal the increasing cracks in the hypothetical wall between markets. Then in a state visit to the FRG in 1987, President Ronald Reagan urged Soviet Premier to accept this loosening of restrictions and aid in the integration of the Soviet bloc into the world system with the famous words "Mr. Gorbachev, tear down this wall!" Though it was 2 more years until the Wall actually fell (under the administration of President George H. W. Bush, Reagan's Vice President), Reagan is usually given credit for the collapse of the GDR and the Berlin Wall. Yet the collapse of the Berlin Wall and the end of the GDR was really the result of intensified pressure from the people trapped behind the wall (Meyer, 2009, pp. 1–14).

Fig. 1.6: Rubik's Cube, c. 1980

The fall of the Berlin Wall is commemorated on November 9, 1989. Yet that was not an isolated event. In September of that year, tens of thousands of East Germans began crossing the border from Hungary to Austria, and onto the FRG (our exhibit features artifacts from one such defector, Uli Meunch). The media dubbed this "The Great Escape." For their part, East Germans divided themselves into two subgroups—stayers and leavers. According to Meyer, some who were determined to stay often perceived the leavers as only interested in making money and were just as worried about what a mass exodus to the FRG would mean for the GDR (Meyer, 2009, pp. 113–126).

The East German government had to do something to alleviate the mounting pressure. During October 1989 several anti-government protests took place in the country including Berlin, Dresden, and Leipzig (Meyer, 2009, pp. 147–161). The answer to these problems was to change leadership—Erich Honecker was out, and Egon Krenz was in as Premier. With a new leader came a new travel policy. On November 9, GDR spokesman Gunter Schabowski prematurely announced a new travel policy relaxing restrictions on GDR citizens to cross the border. Why it was announced when it was to actually happen is still open to debate. Some believe it was

Fig. 1.7: Postcard Commemorating November 10 celebrations.
On loan from David Bolton

a mistake by Schabowski; others believe he purposely announced the new policy to force change. The important thing is that the announcement led to masses of people marching on the Berlin Wall and crossing into West Berlin (Sonnevend, 2016, pp. 57–83). From the media reports and pictures of East and West Germans standing together on top of the Wall November 10, 1989—such as those emblazoned on postcards on display here—it is believed that capitalism defeated socialism and the Cold War was won.

Bibliography

Heller, Deane & Heller, David. (1962). *The Berlin Wall.* New York: Walker and Company.

ISN (ed.). (2019). "Ich bin ein Berliner Speech by US President John F. Kennedy," Primary Resources in International Affairs (PRIA), International Relations and Security Network website. Accessed May 3, 2019, https://www.files.ethz.ch/isn/125399/1160_KennedyIchbin.pdf.

Judt, M. (ed.). (1997). *DDR-Geschichte in Dokumenten* [*GDR History in Documents*]. Berlin, pp. 545–546. Accessed on January 24, 2021 from http://ghdi.ghi-dc.org/sub_document.cfm?document_id=925.

Klein, C. (2019). 10 Things You May Not Know About the Berlin Wall. History.com. November 9. Accessed on January 24, 2021 from https://www.history.com/news/10-things-you-may-not-know-about-the-berlin-wall.

Meyer, M. (2009). *The year that changed the world: The untold story behind the fall of the Berlin Wall.* New York: Scribner.

National Museum of Play. (2019). "Rubik's Cube," *National Toy Hall of Fame* website. Accessed May 3, 2019, https://www.toyhalloffame.org/toys/rubiks-cube.

Richie, A. (1998). *Faust's metropolis: A history of Berlin.* New York: Carroll and Graf Publishers.

Scott, T. (1989). *Thomas Müntzer: Theology and revolution in the German reformation.* London: Macmillan.

Sonnevend, J. (2016). *Stories without borders: The Berlin Wall and the making of a global iconic event.* New York: Oxford University Press.

U.S. Department of State (2019b). "The Berlin Crisis, 1958–1961," Office of the Historian, Bureau of Public Affairs, United States Department of State. Accessed May 3, 2019, https://history.state.gov/milestones/1953-1960/berlin-crises.

U.S. National Archives. (2019). "Decorations, Medals, Ribbons, & Similar Devices," Federal Register, National Archives and Records Administration, accessed May 3, 2019, https://www.federalregister.gov/documents/2006/04/05/06-2854/decorations-medals-ribbons-and-similar-devices#sectno-reference-578.45%20.

CHAPTER 1 A City Divided: The History of the Berlin Wall 17

A City Divided: A Timeline History of the Berlin Wall

May 7, 1945
Nazi Germany surrenders to Allied powers, ending World War II in Europe.

July 17–August 2, 1945:
Partition of Germany

At the Potsdam Conference between the victorious Allies, Germany is partitioned into four zones, each controlled by an Allied power (British, French, American, and the Soviet Union). The capital, Berlin, which fell within the Soviet Union's zone, was likewise partitioned, making West Berlin an oasis of capitalism within Communist-controlled territory. Despite its partition, Berlin shared the same infrastructure such as roads, railroads, and an electrical grid.

April 3, 1948:
Marshall Plan begins delivering aid to West Germany

June 24, 1948:
Soviets begin the Berlin Blockade in an attempt to cut off aid to West Germany

June 26, 1948
Berlin Airlift Begins

May 12, 1949
Berlin crisis ends. USSR re-opens land routes.

May 23, 1949:
West Germany officially becomes a separate country, the Federal Republic of Germany

October 7, 1949:
East Germany officially becomes a separate country, the German Democratic Republic (GDR)

As a response to the Blockade, the Allied Powers organized the Berlin Airlift to carry supplies via airplanes to the people of West Berlin, a difficult feat given the size of the city's population. Crews from the United States, Canada, Australia, South Africa, Great Britain and France flew over 200,000 sorties a year, delivering 12,941 tons of food, fuel and supplies per day. The Soviet Union did not attack for fear of escalating the crisis.

1950s
West Germany is dubbed the "Economic Miracle". East Germans move in record numbers over the border to the FRG.

August 12-13, 1961
The Berlin Wall is built

The GDR believed that stopping the flow of refugees from East to West Berlin was necessary for survival.

August 22-24, 1961
First reported deaths at the Wall

Ida Siekmann jumps out a 4th floor window (Aug. 22); Günter Litfin was shot swimming across the Spree River (Aug. 24)

June 26, 1963
U. S. President John F. Kennedy delivers famous "Ich bin ein Berliner" address.

Reassuring West Germany that they will be protected by the United States, JFK famously says "I am a Berliner". It was directed as much at the Soviet Union as it was at West Berliners. The speech is widely regarded as one of the best-known anti-Communist speeches of the Cold War.

September 16, 1979
Two East German families cross the border in a hot air balloon during the night, in one of the most daring defections of the Cold War.

June 12, 1987
U.S. President Ronald Reagan delivers speech calling for the end of the arms race with the Soviet Union and urging the Soviet Premier, "Mr. Gorbachev, tear down this wall!"

Although it received comparatively little press at the time, it has become one of the best-known speeches of the Cold War.

March 8, 1989
Last recorded death at the Wall, as Winifried Freudenberg falls from a hot air balloon.

May—August 1989
Hungary and Austria begin removing their border fence. 900 East Germans flee through the open border during a "friendship picnic" on August 19.

August 16, 1989
Last recorded successful escape across the Wall.

November 9, 1989
GDR spokesman, Günter Schabowski, announces new travel rules allowing transit from the GDR to FRG.

Many interpreted this as the opening of the border, and tens of thousands rush to the Wall that evening. East German border police, overwhelmed, let them pass.

November 10, 1989
Fall of the Berlin Wall

October 3, 1990
Official unification of Germany

Stephen Darrell/Michael Di Giovine

Fig. 1.8: Timeline of the Berlin Wall.

CHAPTER 2

How the Berlin Wall Was Built

Thomas Haughey, MFA

Although the Berlin Wall is said to have been built in the night of August 12 to 13, 1961, in reality this was just the culmination of a decade of increasingly harsh security measures between East and West Berlin, beginning in 1951 when Soviet premier Josef Stalin called the relatively open border "intolerable" and suggested "The demarcation line between East and West Germany should be considered a border—and not just any border, but a dangerous one . . . The Germans will guard the line of defense with their lives." But it wasn't until 10 years later that Soviet premier Nikita Khrushchev, perceiving the young U.S. President John F. Kennedy as weak, approved the GDR's plan to swiftly construct a wall.

The wall was actually constructed in phases. On August 12 to 13, East German workers quickly dug trenches along the border and erected barbed wire. August 13 became known as "Barbed Wire Sunday." Then, by August 17, they began erecting prefabricated, concrete barriers that were 12 feet high; metal and barbed wire were sometimes put at the top. Later improvements were made between 1965 and 1975, and then the "Fourth Generation Wall" was built between 1975 and 1980. These barriers were L-shaped, so that the cantilever at the bottom would provide counter-weight for protection; if any truck attempted to bash through the wall, the weight of the truck on top of the base would prevent the wall from

Contributed by Thomas Haughey, MFA. © Kendall Hunt Publishing Company

20 CHAPTER 2 How the Berlin Wall Was Built

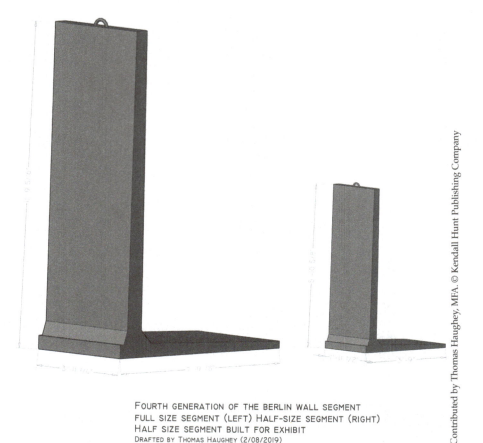

FOURTH GENERATION OF THE BERLIN WALL SEGMENT
FULL SIZE SEGMENT (LEFT) HALF-SIZE SEGMENT (RIGHT)
HALF SIZE SEGMENT BUILT FOR EXHIBIT
DRAFTED BY THOMAS HAUGHEY (2/08/2019)

Fig. 2.1: Berlin Wall schematics

being pushed out. A smooth, rounded pipe was added to the top to make it harder to climb over without falling. Roughly 45,000 pieces were used to make around 100 miles of wall around West Berlin. This version of the wall is the most photographed, and a 1/2 size scale model has been placed at the entrance to the museum, immediately outside Old Library.

But the East Germans didn't just use these segments to create a new wall. Wherever possible, they utilized buildings at the border (including apartment housing and churches), concreting shut the windows. These types of constructions accounted for less than a mile of wall, though. The GDR was careful to make sure that all construction was just inside East Berlin, so the West couldn't justify tearing it down without incident.

Along the longer barrier between East and West Germany, mine fields, chain-linked fences, barbed wire, and trenches were also built.

In June 1962, the GDR government erected a second barrier about 100 meters (113 yards) in front of the wall—a kind-of primary protective barrier. To do this, they destroyed homes and buildings (including, famously, the Church of the Resurrection) to create an empty "no man's land" between the two walls where anyone who tried to cross would be out in the open and able to be easily targeted. This became known as the "death strip."

The wall grew to be reinforced by mesh fencing, signal fencing, anti-vehicle trenches, beds of nails under balconies overhanging

Fig. 2.2: Students Examining the Cantilevered Section of the Berlin Wall at the German Society of Philadelphia

the "death strip" (called "Stalin's Carpet"), guard dogs, some 116 guard towers, and 20 bunkers with hundreds of guards.

It should be noted that the United States and Great Britain largely expected a wall to be built, and even welcomed it. It would stand for both the failure of Communism, as well as the failure of the GDR and Soviet Union to capture all of Berlin. By constructing a wall, the GDR signaled that they had ceased drawing up plans to re-take the entire city. In this way, some theorists think the Wall served a positive purpose, lowering the possibility of nuclear war between the United States and Soviet Union in Europe.

Politics between East and West

Chapter 3: **Behind Enemy Lines: America in West Berlin 1945–1989**
Christopher DiMaria

Chapter 4: **The GDR: A Surveillance State**
Brad Nehls

Chapter 5: **The Stasi, East Germany's Powerful and Secret Intelligence Agency**
Mark Duffy

Chapter 6: **Alfred Cardinal Bengsch: Navigating the Split City of Berlin**
Brenda Gaydosh

Chapter 7: **Escaping East Berlin: The Bethke Brothers**
Chase Fitzgerald

CHAPTER 3

Behind Enemy Lines: America in West Berlin 1945–1989

Christopher DiMaria

Shortly after the Nazi surrender in 1945, the capital city of Berlin was split into four sectors. The eastern part of the city was controlled by the Soviet Union while the west was split into three sectors, which were controlled by the United States, France, and England. Much like Berlin, Germany itself would also be divided into four sectors again with the Soviets controlling the East and the Americans, French and, English controlling the West. In the years following the Second World War, the western territories of Berlin would become the center of a conflict between two superpowers that would become known as the Cold War. West Berlin would become the most important strategic position the Americans had during the beginning of the Cold War and its very existence would bring the world to the brink of nuclear war.

Following World War II, the Americans approached Germany in a very different manner than they had following the First World War. Rather than punish or abandon Germany as they had done after the First World War, the Americans devoted themselves to rebuilding and rehabilitating Germany. By actively trying to rehabilitate Germany, the Americans could all but guarantee that the conditions that allowed the Nazis to take power in Germany following

Contributed by Christopher DiMaria. © Kendall Hunt Publishing Company

World War I would not occur again. The need for America to establish presence and influence in Germany only grew as tensions between the Soviets and Americans grew in the years following World War II. Berlin's location deep within the Soviet-controlled East would make it one of if not the most important strategic positions the Americans had against the Soviets. Because of this, letting it fall into the hands of the Soviets would be likened to letting all of Germany succumb to the Communist threat.

In 1949 the American dedication to Berlin would endure its first true test with the establishment of a Soviet blockade, cutting off all rail and road traffic into West Berlin. The blockade cut off all supply lines coming into West Berlin. Furthermore, the blockade posed a threat to the CIA's intelligence operations in West Berlin (Murphy, 1998, p. 172). West Berlin's location within Soviet territory made it an invaluable location for anti-communist intelligence operations which had been keeping a close eye on the Soviet's development of their own atomic bomb. The blockade made it difficult for anyone to move between East and West Berlin which significantly hampered the CIA's ability to collect intelligence from the East (1998, p. 172). In response to the Soviet blockade, the Americans and English began supplying West Berlin by airlift, flying cargo planes full of supplies into West Berlin 24 hours a day (p. 151). The supplies would be brought into West Berlin for months until the Soviet blockade was lifted. With the effort put forth, it was obvious to the people of West Berlin and the Soviets that America's devotion to West Berlin was cemented.

Following the Berlin Airlift, West Berlin became the focal point of the growing tensions between the Americans and Soviets. Shortly after the end of the airlift, the German Democratic Republic (GDR) was created establishing East Germany as its own nation. The newly established GDR set its sights on West Berlin as the city existence posed a major threat to the new government's integrity. West Berlin's capitalist economy meant that western goods were readily available in West Berlin but not in the East. The GDR was concerned that having this capitalist island within their territory would make their own economic system look undesirable and cause their citizens to flee to the West. The GDR's concerns seem justified, as many of its citizens were, in fact, fleeing from East to

West Berlin. Furthermore, with the Soviets' successful atomic bomb test in August of 1949, the tensions between the Americans and the now-nuclear capable Soviets were growing by the day. Berlin's strategic location continued to provide the CIA with intelligence regarding Soviet and East German operations. The threat of nuclear war and the GDR's desire to unify Berlin under GDR rule meant that West Berlin's existence as an independent entity was more important than ever.

Fig. 3.1: U.S. Intelligence exhibit. EAI PACE TR-10 computer; Briefcase and notebook donated by CIA clandestine officer working in Europe during the Cold War; U.S. Army uniform worn by Lt. Col. Lewis Cressler (ret.) in 1963 Berlin.

28 **CHAPTER 3** Behind Enemy Lines: America in West Berlin 1945–1989

By the late 1950s, the Cold War was in full swing and both the Americans and Soviets possessed nuclear weapons. The number of citizens fleeing the GDR to West Berlin was growing by the day, and the GDR was pressuring Russia to take action. In response,

Fig. 3.2: EAI PACE TR-10. *On loan from The Computer Church*

between 1958 and 1961, the Soviet Union's leader, Nikita Khrushchev, tried in vain to reunite Berlin—even going as far as to say that he would rather fight a nuclear war than give up on Berlin (May, 1998, p. 155). However, the threats proved empty, and a solution to the Berlin problem was far less drastic.

In August 1961, seemingly overnight, a crude wall was constructed around West Berlin. In actuality the wall was constructed over time in stages, starting with concrete blocks; fences, fences, barbed wire, watchtowers, dog runs, searchlights, and a second poured concrete wall would eventually complete what would become known as the Berlin Wall (May, 1998, p. 155). The wall's construction was a response to the mass exodus of East Germans through West Berlin, and was intended to keep the influence of capitalism contained. In many ways, it was a compromise.

After the construction of the wall, intelligence operations conducted by the CIA, would continue. However, Berlin's importance as an intelligence hub was reduced both because of the wall, as

Fig. 3.3: Piece of the Berlin Wall collected by then-Lt. Dana Cressler. See also Fig. 14.2. *On loan from Dana Cressler.*

well as America's focus was turned toward Cuba and Vietnam in the years to follow. Nonetheless, the 1960s brought on a new era for espionage and intelligence gathering with advancements in computer technology. Analog computers used to crack coded messages, like the EAI PACE TR-10 that were manufactured in the early 1960s (Fig. 3.2), proved to be valuable assets for the CIA and the armed forces. Cumbersome analog computers like the TR-10 demonstrated the value that computers could have in intelligence-gathering and paved the way for the digital computers that military uses today.

The wall's existence would span generations for both the Germans living with it and the Americans stationed there. In 1989, as the wall was coming down, a piece of the wall was chipped off by

Fig. 3.4: Frank Trolio, WWII veteran stationed in Berlin in 1945, visits *Faces of the Berlin Wall* with museum director Michael A. Di Giovine

then-Lt. Dana-Cressler—an American soldier and the son of Col. Lewis Cressler, who had been stationed in Berlin in 1961 when the wall was erected (Fig. 3.3). The American flag would fly over the American headquarters in Berlin until 1994, and American troops were stationed in Berlin during the entirety of the Cold War (see Fig. 3.4). The Americans would stay devoted to West Berlin from the end of World War II and even after the wall came down in 1989, defending Berlin likely as they would any American city, and seeing that freedom prevailed even after the GDR collapsed.

Bibliography

May, E. R. (1998). America's Berlin: Heart of the Cold War. *Foreign Affairs, 77*(4): 148–160.

Murphy, D. E. (1998). Spies in Berlin: A hidden key to the Cold War. *Foreign Affairs, 77*(4): 171–178.

CHAPTER 4

The GDR: A Surveillance State

Brad Nehls, Jr.

Marked by spying and the torture of its own people, the GDR was a socialistic/communistic government that built the Berlin Wall to keep people in rather than keeping people out. One hundred and forty souls lost their lives trying to escape over the wall, while many others were jailed and interrogated. The constant surveillance on East Berliners and East German border houses caused husbands and wives, children and parents, and neighbors to spy on each other. The surveillance state of the GDR created a powder keg that slowly began to explode on them, citizens becoming enemies of the state. The GDR's secret police, the Stasi, kept files on the citizens, as well as used informants for spying on those living within East Berlin and along the border. It was their job to keep the citizenry in line and to tow the communist party line. The East Berliners and anyone living close to the border of West Germany saw 40 years of witch hunts, false imprisonments, and torture all for the sake of communism to succeed.

Citizens were forced to spy on one another for a government trying to stop detractors. This created tension between their loved ones and themselves. The Stasi would coerce them, threatening to ruin the lives (Vaizey, 2016). Other citizens, after receiving constant bouts of torture, betrayed friends, and family. An example of being tortured and then betrayed comes from the account by Miriam in the book *Stasiland*, in which the author Anna

Contributed by Brad Nehls. © Kendall Hunt Publishing Company

Funder (2003, pp. 17–18) utilized oral histories from East Germans to reconstruct the terrors of the East German secret police:

> Several days went by. Miriam and Ursula agreed on an arrest and incarceration plan: neither would admit anything. The Stasi arrived at a shortlist of suspects. Men with gloves and dogs combed Miriam's house. 'And we thought we had been so careful, thrown everything out destroyed all the evidence.' The Stasi found some of the little rubber letters in the carpet. Miriam's parents told the officers they did not know how such a thing could happen in their house. Both girls were placed in solitary confinement for a month. They had no visits from their parents or from lawyers, no books, no newspapers, not a phone call. In the beginning, they stuck to their plan. 'No sir, I don't know either how the leaflets got there, no it couldn't possibly have been her.' 'But eventually,' Miriam says, 'they break you. Just like fiction. They used the old trick and told each of us that the other had admitted, so we might as well too. After no visits, no books, nothing, you think 'well, she probably did say it.' The girls were let out to await their trials. When she got home Miriam thought, there's no way they're going to put me back in that place. The next morning she got on a train for Berlin. It was New Year's Eve 1968, and Miriam Weber was going over the Wall.

Miriam proceeded to try to escape from East Berlin and was caught, jailed, and further tortured for almost starting another world war (Funder, 2003, p. 18). These instances of jailing for no more than peacefully wanting to leave or change how the government was run was common in the GDR. Timothy Garton Ash (1990, p. 61) provides another look into the brutality of the Stasi force.

> East German border-guards watched impassively, or rode up and down the death Strip on their army motorbikes. On the morning of Sunday, 12 November I walked through the Wall and across that no man's land with a crowd of East Berliners, a watchtower to our left, Hitler's bunker to our right. Bewildered border-guards waved us through. As recently as February their colleagues had shot dead a man trying to escape.

Ash paints a vivid image to demonstrate how most people of East Berlin were willing to risk death to escape the GDR and Stasi hold over its citizenry. However, there were instances where individuals and their families who did not live close to the border or directly in Berlin were left to live peacefully by the Stasi (Finnin, I., interview 4/10/19). This stark contrast shows that most of the Stasi's attention was on the border of West Germany and West Berlin. Having a divided country and identity would further separate the two sides of the wall into the mentality that the rest of the world was already forming East vs. West.

Being targeted by the Stasi was a realistic possibility that many citizens living in East Berlin lived with daily. The Stasi would open surveillance operations with what was termed the "beginning level," which is designated as personal surveillance operation (OPK) that would wiretap the phone, monitor the mail, and placing informants on the citizen. Once hard evidence came in on the subject, the Stasi would escalate the operation to the next level designated as an operational case (Operativer Vorgang-OV) that would entail greater monitoring and changing from passive monitoring to active involvement (Bruce, 2010, p. 109). These types of surveillance were the main source of information and policing. An East Berliner named Mario provides a glimpse into what the Stasi can do to their citizens when refusing to cooperate or pass information to them (Vaizey, 2016, p. 70):

> Mario, however, declined the Stasi's request, and this is where his problems with the state began. Following his refusal to collaborate, Mario was demoted from his job as a waiter to doing the washing-up. He was also followed by the Stasi. They were blatant about it, he explains. They would get their camera out very ostentatiously so that Mario knew he was being photographed and under observation. It was at this point that I thought even if there's a 90 percent chance that I'll be shot, I want to leave. I can't stand it for one more day, I thought, even if I have to sleep under a bridge in the West it would be better than continuing to live here.

Mario would later be imprisoned for trying to escape. These are but a few examples of the types of recorded surveillance techniques the

Stasi employed on citizens under suspension. This type of surveillance made many East Berliners and East Germans on the border extremely paranoid of their own government. The GDR saw itself as a people's democracy in the intermediate stage of development geared toward a socialist/communist state on the Marxist-Leninist model of government (Heidenheimer & Kommers, 1967). This identification gave the GDR the means to remain in communist control while making itself a surveillance state.

The GDR and Stasi had a contentious relationship with the United States and NATO. The famous story of Horst Hesse is an example of one of these contentious relationships with the United States and NATO. Hess stole two safes from the U.S. headquarters in Berlin and took them across to East Berlin to the GDR as a gift of his "defection." In reality, Hess was a GDR spy who gained access through joining the United States Army as a refugee from the GDR. The GDR then used the incident for propaganda to slander the West Germans, the United States, and NATO (Koehler, 2008). This is but

Fig. 4.1: Stasi exhibit

just one instance of GDR aggression toward the Western world. After the wall fell, the CIA recovered Hess and executed him for espionage. However, with this propaganda being shared, people of East Berlin wrote to their families and friends telling them all the propaganda they have heard with the goal of furthering the discord between East Berliners and the USA and NATO. One example of the type of propaganda spread throughout East Berlin was this statement: "Reagan's policies in this regard are dangerous and built on deception. That scares me. I see him as bearing the chief responsibility for the whole situation" (Strack, 2015). This type of misinformation and propaganda was spread through all of the Eastern Bloc.

The artifacts on display in our exhibit representing the Stasi and how they would have looked at this time, include a recreation of the files used during these instances of surveillance, as well as how these same files were destroyed. The Stasi kept detailed surveillance and operations records in order to track the activities of any possible enemies of the state. These files would contain interrogation and phone call transcripts, intercepted mail, photographs, personal records, and any information that could be used to incriminate a person of interest. After the wall fell in November of 1989, the Stasi began to destroy the millions of files that they had amassed over the years. Stasi officers began by shredding the files, but the sheer amount of paper caused the shredders to fail. As a result, the Stasi resorted to tearing the files by hand or burning them to prevent the files from getting in the hands of the public. When the Stasi headquarters was overrun by protestors in January 1990, the Stasi had left behind over 15,000 sacks containing over 600 million pieces of torn paper. Today a group of about 40 government workers are working to reconstruct the files that the Stasi destroyed. Workers sort through the 600 million pieces and reconstruct them like a never-ending puzzle. An advanced computer that can match up the torn edges is used to quicken the reconstruction process, but it is estimated that it will take over 300 years to successfully reconstruct every piece of paper the Stasi left behind.

Another artifact is an AK-47, a type of firearm that was used to shoot and kill the East Berliners who tried to escape. The Stasi and GDR relied heavily on the AK-47 and started producing their

Fig. 4.2: AK-47 and M-16 on display

own due to its reliability and ease of making (Atlantic Firearms, 2019). The final artifact is a Stasi Border Officer's uniform. They were the officers who gave the orders to shoot the East Berliners trying to escape to the West. The Stasi dress uniform was a copy of the German army uniform used during WWII with the slight change of a light grey jacket used instead of the dark grey for the jacket with the pants remaining the dark grey. The uniform was kept similar to the WWII uniform to indicate Soviet control over East Germany.

The collapse of the wall marked the end of the GDR and the terrible reign of the Stasi. The night of November 9, 1989 will be a night remembered in jubilation by the dissident citizens in East Berlin. At 7:04 p.m., Gunter Schabowski at the end of his press conference gave the news that all East Berlin residence can leave using all the bridge and border crossings to West Berlin. This report created confusion within the Stasi ranks, and when residents began pouring into the streets they could do nothing but confusedly wave people through. This night was the end of the GDR and Stasi regime in East Berlin.

Fig. 4.3: Stasi uniform on display

The Government structure of including socialistic and communistic structure caused the GDR and Stasi to create their own demise. In the end, the contested border became an issue for the GDR government. The role of spying by GDR created heightened paranoia in the citizens trying to plan their escape from the GDR and East Berlin. False imprisonment of citizens and torture only hardened the resolve of the East Berliners who planned to escape. In sum, the constant surveillance and strict rule over the citizens of East Berlin is what contributed to the eventual demise of the GDR and Stasi.

Bibliography

Ash, T. G. (1990). *The magic lantern: The revolution of' '89 witnessed in Warsaw, Budapest, Berlin, and Prague.* New York: Random House.

Atlantic Firearms. (2019). "DDR AK 47 Rifle East German." Atlantic Firearms LLC website. Accessed May 12, 2019. https://owl.purdue.edu/owl/research_and_citation/chicago_manual_17th_edition/cmos_formatting_and_style_guide/web_sources.html.

Bruce, G. (2010). *The firm: The inside story of the Stasi.* New York: Oxford University Press.

Funder, A. (2003). *Stasiland: Stories from behind the Berlin Wall.* New York: Harper Perennial.

Heidenheimer, A. & Kommers, D. P. (1967). *The governments of Germany,* 2nd ed. New York: Thomas Y. Crowell Company.

Koehler, J. O. (2008). *Stasi: The untold story of the East German secret police.* Oxford: Westview Press.

Strack, D. (2015). *Letters over the wall: Life in communist East Germany.* B and L Press.

Vaizey, H. (2016). *Born in the GDR: Living in the shadow of the Wall.* New York, NY: Oxford University Press.

CHAPTER 5

The Stasi, East Germany's Powerful and Secret Intelligence Agency

Mark Duffy

The Ministry for State Security, *Ministerium für Staatssicherheit*, commonly known as the Stasi, was one of the most effective and repressive secret intelligence and police organizations to have ever existed. It had strong ties to the Soviet KGB. The Stasi developed out of the internal security and police apparatus established in the Soviet zone of occupation in Germany after World War II. The agency viewed itself as the "shield and the sword" of the Party and used the symbols for its coat-of-arms (Lemke, 1992, p. 47; Popplewell, 1992, p. 44). This agency was one of the most feared and hated institutions of the East German communist government. The Stasi headquarters complex covered many blocks in Berlin, and the organization had numerous branches throughout the country. Stasi agents detailed their activities in approximately 180 kilometers of shelf space containing files.

The East German legislature passed the law establishing the Stasi on February 8, 1950, 4 months after the creation of East Germany, the German Democratic Republic (GDR). The legislation did not define the formal role of the Stasi, but it was responsible for both domestic political surveillance and foreign espionage

Contributed by Mark Duffy. © Kendall Hunt Publishing Company

(Cameron, 2016). The ruling Socialist Unity Party (SED) oversaw its operations. In the beginning, its staff was very small, and its chief responsibilities were counterintelligence against Western agents and the suppression of any remnants of Nazism. The Stasi faced its first major threat in June 1953 when East German workers revolted against their living conditions and their oppression under the SED. The Stasi failed to quell the uprising, and the Red Army had to suppress the rebellion. Officials removed the head of the Stasi, Wilhelm Zaisser, due to the agency's poor performance in handling the revolt (Popplewell, 1992, p. 40).

After Joseph Stalin's death on March 5, 1953, Nikita Khrushchev put the Stasi under party control. The Stalin regime had employed torture and physical coercion against the adversaries of the Stasi. East Germany faced the unique problems of having its borders with a democratic German state and having West Berlin within its own borders. The Berlin Wall helped to alleviate some problems with security, but the GDR wanted better security, which it achieved by the maintenance of the Stasi. The particularly harsh measures that the Stasi employed to assure its goals and control included the death penalty, overtly long prison sentences, or the kidnapping of dissidents. The Communist party under Khrushchev eliminated physical repression but did not trust all citizens within the country. Therefore, it used the Stasi to collect information on people (Popplewell, 1992, p. 41). The Stasi had a primary duty of ensuring that only citizens loyal to the Party received good or important jobs and those disloyal got the worst positions. The Stasi sometimes acted as an agent of overt repression when the need arose (p. 41). From 1956 to 1957, the organization subdued student opposition in East Berlin; in 1960, it helped with the ruthless collectivization of agriculture; in 1972, it assisted in the nationalization of East Germany's last privately owned businesses. The Stasi successfully achieved its goal of spying on foreign governments. The discovery in April 1972 that one of West German Chancellor Willy Brandt's top aides was an East German spy forced Brandt to resign.

Erich Mielke became the director of the Stasi in 1957 and remained in that position until its collapse in 1989. Under his leadership, the Stasi sought to infiltrate every societal institution and all aspects of daily life, including personal and familial relationships. To help the agency accomplish these goals, the Stasi relied on its staff and a vast network of informants and unofficial collaborators, who spied on and denounced friends, neighbors, and family. By 1989, the Stasi had 500,000 to 2,000,000 collaborators and 100,000 employees, which provided information on approximately 6,000,000 East German citizens, more than one-third of the population (Lemke, 1992, p. 49). The agency divided its informers into various categories. The most important were the *Inoffizielle Mitarbeiter* (unofficial employees) or IM and the *Gesellschaftliche* (social employees of Security or GMS). The GMS was a lower form of the IM. The IM were not just informers but also agents of Party influence in society.

The Stasi's physical resources were just as large as its personnel resources. In 1989, its budget was 3.6 billion Ostmarks, amounting to 1.3% of the state budget. Of this amount, the agency spent 2.4 billion Ostmarks on personnel and 1.2 billion Ostmarks on building, technology, equipment, energy, and fuel (Popplewell, 1992, p. 45). The Stasi had over 2,037 installations, 652 of which were in Berlin. The organization also had a stockpile of weapons second only to the army and its own 10,992-strong elite regiment, the Felix Dzerzhinsky Guards. This personal army guarded installations of the Party and State leadership, and other security and representative tasks (see Koch & Lapp, 2008).

In the 1970s, Mielke's promotion to the Politburo gave him greater opportunities to influence political decisions of the Stasi. After Mikhail Gorbachev became the leader of the Soviet Union in 1985, Mielke suppressed the growing influence of his perceived political opponents, amounting to wholesale surveillance (Popplewell, 1992, p. 43). By the spring of 1986, the Stasi realized that it could no longer rely on the Red Army if serious unrest occurred in East Germany. The officials therefore increased internal spying. Regular Stasi officers, known as officers on special assignment, infiltrated key positions in the state and economy to protect important information and property from hostile forces. For the first time, the Stasi spied on the Party itself. The Stasi sought to control all forms of communication between the two German states, including private meetings, telephone conversations, and the flow of books, journals, and letters. Human rights and peace activists reported that repression increased in the

1980s. This occurred because the ultimate goal was to establish a perfect espionage network that covered every citizen in the GDR (pp. 43–44).

The Stasi fell when the East German regime collapsed. Prior to the March 18, 1990 election in East Germany, in which voters overwhelming backed unification with West Germany, criticism escalated against the Stasi. One election poster (see Center for History and New Media, 2007), shows the popular sentiment toward the Stasi when the Berlin Wall fell. Against a black frame, it presents what appears to be a face made of two buttons, and an X out of bandages for a silenced mouth. In the center—where the nose would be—are the words: "GEGEN STARRSINN UND KORRUPTION", or "Against Pig-Headedness and Corruption." The letters are all in black except for five letters in red (as denoted by the italics above), which spell out "Stasi." Below the face is the number "18", which alludes to the upcoming ballot. The poster urges voters to vote for a regime change, against a government that spied on itself and its citizens. The East German government destroyed many Stasi files during its last year of government because they contained volumes of damaging information (Lemke, 1992, pp. 51–52). However, citizen groups helped to preserve most of the Stasi files, which accompanied the GDR into united Germany.

Bibliography

Cameron, J. (2016). Stasi. *Britannica online encyclopedia.* Accessed September 20, 2019. https://www.britannica.com/print/article/563751

Center for History and New Media (2007). Making the history of 1989, Item #654. *Center for History and New Media, George Mason University.* Accessed September 20, 2019. http://chnm.gmu.edu/1989/items/show/654

Koch, H. and P. Lapp (2008). *Die Garde des Erich Mielke—Der militärisch-operative Arm des MfS—Das Berliner Wachregiment "Feliks Dzierzynski".* Aachen: Helios-Verlag.

Lemke, C. (1992). Trials and tribulations: 'The Stasi' legacy in contemporary German politics. *German Politics & Society, 26* (Summer): 43–53.

Popplewell, R. (*1992*). The Stasi and the East German revolution of 1989. *Contemporary European History, 1*(1): 37–63.

CHAPTER 6

Alfred Cardinal Bengsch: Navigating the Split City of Berlin

Brenda Gaydosh

Fig. 6.1: Alfred Cardinal Bengsch

In 1950, Cardinal Konrad von Preysing, outspoken Catholic bishop in Berlin against the Nazis in the 1930s and 1940s, ordained Alfred Bengsch a priest. Father Bengsch taught at the seminary in Erfurt (under Soviet control in the East) and continued his studies, earning a PhD in 1956. The Vatican named Bengsch auxiliary bishop of Berlin in 1959. Given the continued persecution of Catholics in the German Democratic Republic (DDR), the Church decided to place Bengsch in the East. Alfred Bengsch was quite intelligent and seemed to know how to deal with the "enemy." He also had lived and studied in the East. He found out quickly what being the highest Church leader in East Berlin entailed.

Within a few months, the Stasi (the official state security in the DDR) bugged the telephone line in Bengsch's apartment. The bishop had been suspicious of the men installing his telephone line, and he asked a friend from West Berlin, a telegraph office official to stop by and look at what the men had installed. His friend found a "bug" and cut the wire. Very quickly, two Stasi agents took Bengsch and his friend in for questioning. One of the agents told Bengsch that the authorities had a good deal of incriminating evidence of illegal Catholic activities in the DDR (Schaeffer, 2010, p. 71). The Stasi also indicated to Bengsch that Cardinal Julius Döpfner had not been willing to work with the State and that was why he could not accomplish anything in the DDR. It was somewhat a shot over the bough for the new bishop. Bengsch should be "realistic" about the situation. Ultimately, it appears that Bishop Bengsch (and later Cardinal Bengsch) worked within the system. It may have left a bad taste in his mouth at times, but it was best for the Church and for his Catholic congregations. At the same time, the Stasi sidestepped the issue of the "bug," trying to blame the listening device on American and British secret agents (the listening device was British-made).

On Sunday, October 18, 1959, Bengsch was celebrating the sacrament of Confirmation with one of his congregations. The Stasi reported,

> Since Confirmation can be celebrated only with a bishop, Bishop Dr. Alfred Bengsch appeared. In his confirmation homily before about 100 confirmands, he said, "It would be only a blessing." In my opinion, it was also understood that the Catholic Church is against the Jugendweihe and was reinforced through these words. He conducted further that the last step of the Confirmation

was communion and with that, Confirmation was complete. In his homily he said, "that we are surrounded by unbelievers and that it only would be a blessing. There should exist the confirmation true to the Church" (Stasi Archives, 1992c, p. 24).

In August 1961, only 3 days after workers had begun construction of the Berlin Wall, the Vatican moved Döpfner to Munich and named Alfred Bengsch the bishop of Berlin. Bishop Bengsch, the new ecclesiastical leader, had to prepare to navigate a split city and negotiate with demons. Bengsch and his staff did not know exactly how the wall might change Catholic life in Berlin. Within days, Prelate Zinke went to the Minister for State Security and requested that Bishop Bengsch have access to West Berlin and that all bishops in the DDR continue to participate in the Fulda Bishops' Conference (Stasi Archives, 1992c, p. 87). Would there be a quid pro quo? *Naturlich!* (Naturally!)

On August 24, a CDU (Christian Democratic Union Party) official told the bishop that no permits for travel to the West were possible, but that in the future the DDR State Council would reward "loyal" responses regarding the new wall. In an internal note, Bishop Bengsch wrote, "I could never speak out in approval of [the wall]. Our ministerial efforts aim to calm the community. Toleration from the state would be very welcome from our perspective, but the State Council must know that souls cannot be bought" (Stasi Archives, 1992c, p. 87). As German Catholic leaders had done under Bismarck's *Kulturkampf* and under the Reich Concordat with the Nazis, Bengsch would have to show the State that his interests lay with ministering to his Catholic flock and that he had no interest in the politics of the DDR. Beginning in September 1961, Bengsch was able to travel to West Berlin on a "case by case" basis.

His inaugural homilies showed that he was not going to be critical of the East's Communist regime. Denying Bengsch access to West Berlin's Catholics could be counterproductive. Yet, the Stasi would have to watch him. A report from September 23, 1961 noted the personality of Bengsch: "Because he is a truly strong personality, it will be difficult. He will not be intimidated by threats or danger, nor can he be tripped up by certain tricks we have at our disposal" (Schaeffer, 2010, p. 85). A Stasi document from 1963 notes that

"2 days" per month in West Berlin would be enough for Bengsch to have contact with West German bishops and care for his institutions (Stasi Archives, 1992b, p. 89). As time passed, Bengsch was allowed to visit the western sector 3 days each month, then 4, and then 10. Every evening, he had to return to East Berlin (Anon, 1980, p. 7).

The bishop not only had to think about his schedule of service to his people, but also, given the Wall, he had to think about the people themselves. All of the bishops serving the Church in the DDR came together with a statement for their people. On the last Sunday of October 1961, a pastoral letter from the Berlin Conference of bishops was read in Berlin Churches; it was an attempt to calm the people:

> More pressing than ever before, we bishops perceive in the present hour the admonition of God: Comfort, comfort my people.... Be assured that we will suffer through with you, everything that disheartens you. We need, therefore, not to repeat what we have often said in the last two years; we need not to depict what you experience and what we experience immediately. Our comfort cannot persist in that we belittle the grave burdens. The dilemma in which many of you find yourselves prohibits every poor attempt of pacification. The concerns that torture your souls are not waved aside with few a few optimistic words ... (Anon, 1980, pp. 52, 54).

Bishop Bengsch realized that he needed to be the voice for the Catholic Church and if other voices joined the chorus, he might find himself cut off below the knees. Within the BOK (Berlin Conference of Ordinaries), Bengsch tried to limit all "political" conversations with state officials, which included the State Secretariat for Church Affairs, the Ministry of Foreign and Inner-German Trade, and the Stasi to himself or his staff and yet, there were plenty of reports on Bengsch by the Stasi:

> (1959) Political evolution: Bengsch studied at the seminary in Fulda and philosophy and theology in Munich. He was ordained April 2, 1950 and became chaplain at Herz Jesu in Berlin in 1954 ... Bengsch is the right hand of Cardinal Döpfner in the pursuit of clerical-anti-democratic

CHAPTER 6 Alfred Cardinal Bengsch: Navigating the Split City of Berlin

deeds of the Catholic Church against the DDR (Stasi Archives, 1992c, p. 4).

(1964) In the preparation and during the Second Vatican Council, Bengsch played an active role. The relevance of Bengsch in connection to the Second Vatican Council exists primarily in that he, through his politics against the government of the DDR, not only gathered certain expert knowledge for the reaction of the Catholic Church under socialist conditions, but also this knowledge generalized formulations of definite submittals for the Council (Stasi Archives, 1992b, p. 60).

(1966) Bengsch reads with predilection detective novels; he lived with the sisters in Gürtelstraße; one of the sisters exercises a great influence with Bengsch (Stasi Archives, 1992b, p. 16).

(1969) From IM "Brunhilde": She recognizes B from youth and childhood. B went to school in the Höchste Str., he belonged to St. Pius. His parents . . . in their 30s . . . later, they went to the West. They did not support the Nazis. B was a daredevil, they played football and went swimming. He was an open Berlin youth. He wore a belt with (symbol chi rho shown) later he came to his occupation. B is now (blacked out) ill. He suffers from (blacked out) (Stasi Archives, 1992d, p. 1).

In June 1967, Pope Paul VI named Alfred Bengsch "Cardinal." This was perhaps a political move on the part of the Vatican. Bengsch was the first East German named Cardinal. It would go a long way perhaps in improving relations between Church and State in the DDR—at a higher level at least. Stasi officials did not limit their surveillance and investigations now that Bengsch received the "red hat."

Stasi officials did not look simply for actions against the state; they imagined actions against the state. There was paranoia within the Stasi ranks. Any Church gathering or affair was somehow an attack against the DDR and its ideology. Officials could not conceive that participation in the Second Vatican Council was simply participation in a Church Council. Catholicism was international and yet, the Stasi and some leaders of the DDR viewed Church activities as a particular attack on communism.

52 **CHAPTER 6** Alfred Cardinal Bengsch: Navigating the Split City of Berlin

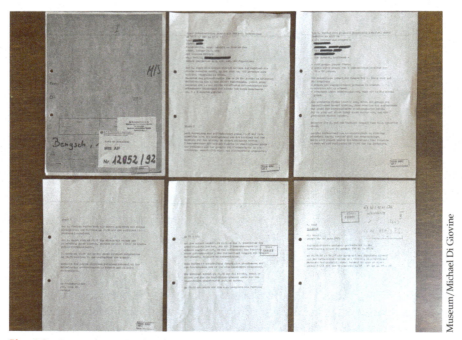

Fig. 6.2: Pages from Cardinal Bengsch's Stasi file

In the 1920s, the Papal Nuncio, Eugenio Pacelli (who would later become Pope Pius XII), had concluded several region concordats in German as a way of safeguarding German Catholic life. In 1933, the Reich Concordat gave the Catholic Church a document to refer to when Catholic practice in Germany was threatened. As time passed, in the DDR in the 1960s, some thought that it was perhaps time for a concordat between state and Church. Cardinal Bengsch, however, knew that a concordat between the DDR and the Vatican would make things worse (Stasi Archives, 1992b, p. 3). In a sense, Bengsch's communications with Secretary Ulbricht were a living, active concordat. Bengsch negotiated; he brought attention to persecution against Catholic practice; he kept negotiations simple.

DDR officials had allowed Bengsch to travel to West Berlin, but he could not always minister to the western flock as he could the eastern flock. DDR officials viewed Bengsch's visits to West Berlin as a favor, a favor that they could rescind if he did anything to provoke the socialist state. In May 1969, State Secretary Hans

Seigewasser ascertained that "State relations to Bengsch and the Catholic Church had 'stiffened,' and consequently, he would strengthen regional efforts and limit Cardinal Bengsch's travel to West Berlin" (Schaefer, 2010, p. 106). There were times throughout his two decades in Berlin that Bengsch uttered something that the State did not like and it punished him by disallowing his monthly visits to West Berlin. The State used West Berlin in a carrot and stick exercise. They kept reports on Bengsch's travels to West Berlin—his aims in going to West Berlin and what he actually did when he was there.

Not only did Bengsch travel to West Berlin for special services or meetings with brother bishops, but he also had contact with political leadership in the West. In 1965, the West German government considered blocking certain money transfers to reduce the DDR's access to Western currency. These transfers were important in maintaining Church institutions in the East. Bengsch requested that Bonn keep the trade route open. He declared that the transfer of funds made it possible to keep negotiations with the SED State down to a minimum (Schaefer, 2010, p. 121). In October 1966, Bengsch asked the papal nuncio in Bonn (the capital of West Germany) to consider adjusting diocesan borders to reflect the DDR-Poland border. Bengsch asserted, "What can today appear as purely a church decision might tomorrow look like a political measure with consequences that are difficult to predict" (p. 136).

The economics of the West versus the East helped Bengsch to negotiate for Church needs in West Berlin. The DDR had need of Western currency, and it listened to Bengsch in 1961 when he asked for the construction of a new building behind St. Hedwig's. Bengsch had offered 1.1 million DM from West Germany for the construction of the building. The DDR could not handle the construction at the time and withheld its approval of the project. Nevertheless, the building was constructed 6 years later with a bit of overcharging of West Germany. Bengsch knew when to speak and when to remain silent.

Historically, the Catholic Church in Germany was to remain silent on political matters. The Pulpit Paragraph, instituted in Germany in 1871 as part of her criminal code, said that the state could imprison a clergyman for up to 2 years for speaking about political matters from the pulpit. This law was still on the books during the Nazi era, and there were Catholic priests imprisoned under this law. The Gestapo imprisoned Father Bernhard Lichtenberg, Provost of St. Hedwig's Cathedral in Berlin, for 2 years because he had prayed for the Jews. Nazis viewed the prayers as a political move against their ideology. For the Church under communism, silence could be golden. Following the building of the Berlin Wall, Bengsch "repeatedly signaled to state officials that the Catholic Church would practice strict 'political abstinence' regarding comments on SED politics. . . . For the state, this silence counted as 'loyalty'" (Schaefer, 2010, p. 277). Nevertheless, the term "political" was a moving target. For the Godless communists, Catholic sacraments and prayer could appear "political."

Cardinal Bengsch was serious about the "silence." Prior to an East German synod of Bishops in Dresden's Hofkirche in March 1973, a lay Catholic involved in the Synod noted, "The Cardinal is having a panic attack about the synod. He fears it may produce difficulties for our relation to the state and difficulties for the bishops, the church, and the unity of the Catholic Church in the DDR" (Schaefer, 2010, p. 210). Earlier in the year, Bengsch realized that the Vatican might cut his legs out from under him. In 1972, West Germany had ratified treaties with the USSR and Poland, and the DDR began to plan a diplomatic initiative with the Vatican (p. 180). Similar to Pope Leo XXIII sidestepping the Center Party in the 1870s to negotiate more directly with Chancellor Bismarck, it seemed that the Vatican wanted to begin serious diplomatic relations with the DDR. The Vatican told Cardinal Bengsch that the DDR was pressuring it for continued talks, but Bengsch and others did not observe such "pressure." Talks continued at the high level, but direct diplomatic relations did not take place.

Much of what Cardinal Bengsch had to deal with was a "game." Dealings at a higher level with the Vatican or even the General Secretary (Walter Ulbricht or Erich Honecker) were important. To help reunite families, to continue the life of the seminaries, to participate in Bishops Congresses, etc. were significant issues to negotiate. Yet, when one looks at what the Stasi was doing, it seems like busy work. Stasi officials followed individuals, listened in on everyday conversations, noted the acquaintances of individuals, and instituted an unofficial spy network that reported on everyday nonsense. Even at the end of Bengsch's life, the Stasi had its eyes focused on those mourning the Cardinal's death.

Cardinal Bengsch had been ill for a while and by mid-1979, he knew that his death was imminent. Thinking ahead, he decided that he wanted to have his body taken one last time to the western sector of Berlin—to be laid out in St. Matthews Church in Berlin-Schöneberg—to be returned in the evening to East Berlin and to have the funeral the next morning at St. Hedwig's. The final day resembled what Bengsch wanted (Anon, 1980, p. 7). The participation of the people at the death of the cardinal was moving and the Stasi was there to watch it all. In the Stasi archives, one can find photographs taken outside St. Hedwig's Cathedral, hand-drawn maps of St. Hedwig's inside and outside, documents covering the funeral. The Stasi assigned individuals to cover rooms in the Cathedral, locations outside the Cathedral, and streets near the Cathedral (Stasi Archives, 1992a, 3–7, 48–49). Stasi records show that 1,034 Stasi agents and 395 police were deployed, and six detention points were set up in case of mass arrest (Schaefer, 2010, p. 202). Ultimately, Alfred Cardinal Bengsch's body was buried, uprising free, in St. Hedwig's Cathedral and the Stasi prepared for the new bishop—Joachim Meisner. Meisner was not as "predictable" as Bengsch to whom the Stasi had become accustomed and the Church had lost its dominating personality in Berlin.

Bibliography

Anon. (1980). *Bengsch, Alfred: Der Kardinal aus Berlin*. Berlin: Morus-Verlag.

Schaefer, B. (2010). *The East German state and the Catholic Church, 1945–1989*. (J. Skolnik & P. C. Sutcliffe, Trans.). New York: Berghahn Books.

Stasi Archives (1992a). MfS AP, Nr. 11283/92

Stasi Archives (1992b). MfS AP, Nr. 11284/92

Stasi Archives (1992c). MfS AP, Nr. 12065/92

Stasi Archives (1992d). MfS Karteikarte BV Bln Abt. XX-AK1

CHAPTER 7

Escaping East Berlin: The Bethke Brothers

Chase Fitzgerald

When Germany split into the Allied-controlled West and the Soviet Union–controlled East after World War II, each side created governments in resemblance of the countries that backed them. The West created a capitalist system while the East created a communist society due to influence from Joseph Stalin and the Soviet Union. The East German government faced many problems, with its biggest one being the wave of emigration out of East Germany to the West with 1.65 million people leaving by 1961. (The people "voted with their feet.") Walter Ulbricht, a prominent leader in the East German government understood that East Germany needed to do something to keep her citizens in if she had any hope of successfully running a country. Therefore, in 1961, East Germany began construction of the Berlin Wall in order to prevent any more people from leaving. She did everything she could to make the wall as hard as possible to get through by including minefields, barbed wire, and guards stationed at various points to keep watch. However, despite these measures, some people were still able to cross over into West Germany, including the Bethke brothers who instigated not one, not two, but three successful escapes from East Berlin.

The first of the brothers to escape was Ingo Bethke, the oldest. Fourteen years after the wall went up, Ingo signed up to join the

Contributed by Chase Fitzgerald. © Kendall Hunt Publishing Company military in East Berlin and patrolled a portion of the border along the Elbe River. After serving, Ingo and one of his friends decided to flee East Berlin through the same part of the border at which he used to be stationed, using his knowledge from when he was a guard. Although there was no wall at this portion of the border, there were many obstacles that they had to overcome. There was a metal fence that had barbed wire covering it, as well as a trip wire that would notify the guards if either of them touched it. After getting through the fence using wire cutters and carefully making their way over the trop wires, Ingo had to pass a field of mines that protected the river while evading guards the entire time. He managed to navigate his way through the mine field using a small paddle that had a long enough handle where if the paddle set off a mine, he would be at a far enough distance to avoid serious injury. After getting through the mine field without setting off a single mine, one task remained: crossing the river. The river had a very strong current that made it very difficult to swim across. To avoid being swept away by the river and possibly drowning, Ingo blew up an air mattress and quietly paddled the 164 yards to West Berlin, successfully accomplishing an incredibly daring escape.

Eight years after Ingo left, his younger brother, Holger, waited for his moment and finally figured out a way to reunite with his older brother. After every successful escape attempt, the Soviet border patrol investigated and added additional security measures to prevent similar escapes from happening again. Therefore, Holger could not escape the same way Ingo had. The fence now had an electric current running through it to prevent people from using wire cutters, and a bed of nails was now added between the wall and the fence to make matters even more difficult. This made getting through the barriers virtually impossible. Therefore, instead of going through the barriers, Holger came up with a different strategy. He had been practicing archery over the years and had concocted a plan to zipline over the wall with Ingo's help. There was a portion of the wall that had a tall building only 40 meters away from it and one night, Holger climbed to the top and put his archery skills to use by shooting an arrow with a nylon line tied to it over the wall to the awaiting Ingo on the other side. Ingo tied the line to the back of his car and drove a couple meters and pulled the rope as tight as possible to make sure Holger had enough momentum to make it over the wall. Holger tied his end to his chimney

CHAPTER 7   Escaping East Berlin: The Bethke Brothers

and using a metal pulley, attempted to zipline over the wall, but lost his momentum about three yards away from the other side. Holger then grabbed the wire and acrobatically climbed the remaining distance to the other side safe and soundly, successfully reuniting with his brother Ingo.

Fig. 7.1: WCU's memorial to those fallen trying to escape East Berlin

Ingo and Holger moved to the city of Cologne and started a successful bar there, but there was one problem: their brother, Egbert, was still stuck in West Berlin. They were having trouble coming up with a plan to get him out when they stumbled upon a new aircraft called the "ultralight," which was a tiny plane that was easy to transport and could land in small spaces. The two brothers learned to fly the ultralight and 6 years after Holger's escape, they were ready to enact their plan. The brothers painted their planes with red stars to avoid drawing any suspicion from the border guards or to at least buy them time as they knew that Soviet guards could not shoot at aircrafts without permission. The time that it would take for the guards to get this permission was more than long enough for Ingo and Holger to pick up Egbert and make their escape. They had been planning this for 4 years and had picked out a small field for them to quickly land and pick up Egbert before anyone could figure out what was going on. At 4:15 a.m. on May 26, 1989, the two brothers set off in two planes and went to pick up Egbert. When Ingo began to land, Egbert quickly ran out of his hiding place and made a break to the plane, where Ingo handed him a helmet and they took off before anyone was the wiser. They swiftly cleared the wall and landed safely on the other side, successfully reuniting with their brother who Holger had not seen in 6 years and Ingo had not seen in 14. The whole escape took no more than 30 minutes and capped off the incredible story of the Bethke Brothers accomplishing three times what most failed to accomplish once.

Escaping was not as easy as the Bethke brothers made it out to be. Hundreds of people died trying to make it over, under, or through the wall, with each successful escape making it tougher for others to cross over, due to the border patrol consistently fixing holes in their security. This forced people to become more creative and to concoct more own ways to get over to the other side. For instance, in 1964, a group of West Germans dug a secret tunnel under the wall and was able to smuggle out an incredible 57 East Germans. In 1979, two families were able to make it over the wall by using a secretly made hot air balloon. This shows how strong the will of the German people is as it is something that no barrier, government, or wall can contain.

Bibliography

Halmburger, O. (2009). *Busting the Berlin Wall: Amazing escape stories*, performed by Clayton Nemrow. Germany: History Channel (TV).

Heller, D. F. & Heller, D. (1962). *The Berlin Wall*. New York: Walker and Company.

"Rise and Fall of the Berlin Wall," *History Channel.*

Steege, P. (2011). Ordinary violence on an extraordinary stage: Incidents on the sector border in postwar Berlin. *Performances of Violence*, 140–163.

Lived Experiences

Chapter 8: Globalization and the East-West Divide
Emily Rodden and Jacqueline Wanjek

Chapter 9: Tourism and Mobility in the Eastern Bloc
Michael A. Di Giovine, Ph.D.

Chapter 10: Divided Germany, Divided Sports
Jenna Walmer

Chapter 11: Through Their Eyes
Margaret Hartnett

Chapter 12: Connections: Memoirs of an American Historian in the Communist East Bloc
Claude Foster; edited by Brenda Gaydosh

Chapter 13: Tears in Bitterfeld
Claude Foster

Chapter 14: New Year's Eve, 1989
Dana Cressler

CHAPTER 8

Globalization and the East-West Divide

Emily Rodden and Jacqueline Wanjek

Soon after the end of WWII, Berlin and Germany would be separated into four quadrants of power—American, English, French, and Soviet. Germany was absolutely devastated after the war, but the Allied Forces were worried about Germany rebuilding and re-establishing its power.

After WWII, the chances for German economic recovery were slim; manufacturing plants were completely destroyed. The Allied Control Council prohibited the production of heavy machinery, heavy tractors, aluminum components, radio transmitters, and sea vessels (Hachtmann, 2009). The physical landscape was in ruins, and the economic landscape likewise was destroyed—leaving the Reichsmark virtually worthless (Taylor, 2008). Soon after Germany's partition, the United States instituted the Marshall Plan in Europe, which rebuilt West Germany (FRG) under Western capitalist ideals. In 1948, Reichsmarks were withdrawn and the Deutschmark was introduced to the German economy as a part of the Marshall Plan, completely renovating the West German economy. The Americans and the French issued everyone 40 Deutsche Marks and created purchasing power overnight. By the 1950s West Germany had been dubbed an "economic wonder," or *"wirtschaftswunder"* (Hachtmann, 2009).

The same day the West announced the new D-Marks into Berlin, the Russian-occupied sector took drastic measures. The trains were deliberately rerouted to pass by West Berlin, civilian road traffic had been banned, and travelers were held up for long periods of time in the interzonal border areas (Taylor, 2008). Days after the currency reform, Russia said all links between the western zones had been closed until further notice. This began the Berlin Blockade, arguably creating the first physical divisions between East and West.

West Germany provided ideal conditions for the expansion of economic growth. The West German market quickly developed an urban middle-class; 55% of the population was now able to spend much of its disposable income on consumer durables such as cars and electric goods. Post-war luxuries turned into mass consumption items. While the FRG benefited from the Marshall Plan, it took more than monetary aid to develop a functioning democratic society based on a capitalist system (Hachtmann, 2009).

The creation of two states within Germany, especially the division of the capital of Berlin, formed distinct economies which affected the lived experiences of many people. Two exhibits—one west of

Fig. 8.1: Western and West German products

the wall and one to the east—feature objects that together represent these economic differences between the two states, and illustrate cultural similarities and differences in this time period. For example, despite its modernization, West Germany could produce and sell many of the same products as they could before the war. In addition, unlike the East, West Germans also had access to more globalized products and could compete on a national scale, since it was occupied by three Allied Nations. West Germans were able to purchase major international products like Marlboro cigarettes, Levi Jeans, and Coca Cola—all of which are still common sights in today's global society. However, these were not available in the East, which was dominated by the Soviet Union and had a much weaker economy unable to compete with the West. Indeed, the State typically required both parents to work in order to maintain a stable income (Braun, Scott, & Alwin, 1994). Consequently, the paucity of goods in the East led to a desire to obtain Western products through parcels from families on the other side and/or the black market.

The western exhibit features various items that connect what was available in West Germany during the Cold War with common objects from today. For example, Marlboro, an American brand of cigarettes, became popular in the 1960s and was brought to West Germany (Flaherty, 1987), where it saw success from soldiers and in the black market. Since East Germans in the GDR could not enjoy these cigarettes, American soldiers would buy them at local drugstores in the United States or West Germany for $5 and sell them in the East German black market for around $100 (Ruffner, 2002). Levi Jeans are also featured. They, too, were available in the FRG and not in the GDR, and when they were, they cost far more. In order to stop the circulation of capitalist products through the GDR, jeans like these were banned and alternative brands were created, but they could not compete with western brands in quality (Roppelt, 2014). In 1978, 800,000 Levi Jeans were shipped to the GDR for an average cost of 149 East German marks (about $300 today). Even Coca-Cola was banned in the GDR (Connolly & Gunther 2002) and could only be obtained through the black market. Aware of this, the GDR created Vita Cola to replace Coca-Cola to appease the citizens. Vita Cola is one of a few Eastern products that managed to survive after the reunification, and today it is a competitor with Coca-Cola in Germany.

Fig. 8.2: Soviet and East German products

East Germany was disconnected from the West (see, for example, Hauser, 2006), but that did not mean it was alone in the world. Hungry, Bulgaria, and Czechoslovakia (among others) all were part of the so-called Eastern bloc, under the strong political influence of the Soviet Union to help solidify the bond between the countries within its sphere of influence, the Soviet Union attempted to foster a common Communist identity through its products, TV shows, media, and toys such as those on display in the exhibit to the east.

When the Wall fell, many companies on the East struggled to compete with companies on the West. Like many Eastern companies Ruhal, an East German watch company, could not survive capitalism and closed in 1990. Toy cars are also displayed, representing common East German brands. The Chaika as well as the Trabant were both popular in the East and were cheaper and easier to get than Western cars. However, this did not mean they were affordable. Most people waited 12 years for a car. After reunification these cars were not worth the material they were built with, as they were of a far lower quality than Western cars were (Chapple, 2017; Gureev, n.d.; Hamer & Hamer, 2018). Finally, *Sibylle*, or the "*Vogue* of the East," showcased a very particular type of woman. Fashion was important to East German youth because the state may have dictated where they could shop, learn, and work but they could not dictate how they dressed. This magazine is interesting in many ways because it juxtaposes the Western ideals of the skinny, well-manicured women with the hard working educated women celebrated in the East.

One of the few Eastern products to thrive after the fall of the wall (Wiedemann, 2003; see also Cichanowicz, 2016) was the Sandmann doll. During the Cold War, both children on the East and West watched the Sandmann on TV before bed but the Sandmen were very different from each other. The East's Sandmann—which is on display here (Fig. 8.3)—was seen on TV first in 1959 and still

Fig. 8.3: Sandmann Doll (East Germany) and Barbie Doll (West Germany)

runs today. The East Sandmann captured the hearts of all German children after reunification because his appearance was more child friendly (Hupertz, 2008; Kleiner, 2017). Another successful toy—although apparently not invented for kids' leisure enjoyment (Wallop, 2014)—was the Rubik's Cube, which helped to solidify the bond between socialist countries because it was invented in Hungary and could be traded much easier on the East than in Western countries (see Fig. 1.6). In 1974 Erno Rubik was a professor in Hungary and wanted his students to understand how to solve 3D problems better. The puzzle became a hit and was sold worldwide in 1980 (Rubiks, n.d.).

In line with socialist teachings of equality, the East did provide more rights for women in the workplace and in society. It was much easier to be a single mother in East Germany than it was in West Germany. Unlike the West, which in many places was also dominated by teachings of the Catholic and Lutheran churches, it was easier for women in the East get a divorce. Women were encouraged to continue their career even after becoming mothers. We see examples of this from John Boneman's *Grenzregime: The Wall and its Aftermath* (1998). Boneman talks to a woman named Heidi who grew up in East Germany but now lives in West Germany. Heidi gives examples from her love life and education on how the East and West differ. Heidi talks about her different romances, her education, and life as a single mother. She is grateful for the education and career advances that the East gave her but was aware that, overall, the West likely had more to offer.

When the wall fell, West Germans rushed to the East to buy cheaper land and businesses. Although some West Germans have argued that their government spent too much tax money developing the East, some East Germans complained that they were forced out of their business by more powerful, and globally connected, West German businesses. Such cultural and economic divisions continue today.

Bibliography

Aminova, D. (2017). Korney Chukovsky: The children's author who wrote against all odds. *Russia Beyond* website. Accessed on January 26, 2021 from https://www.rbth.com/arts/literature/2017/03/31/korney-chukovsky_729098

Anon. (2015). "Germany: East German little sandmann." *National Costume Dolls* blog. August 5. Accessed on January 26, 2021 from https://babogenglish.wordpress.com/2015/08/05/germany-east-german-little-sandmann-sandmannchen/

Boneman, J. (1998). *Grenzregime* (Border Regime). In Thomas M. Wilson & Hastings Donnan (eds.). *Border Identities: Nation and State at International Frontiers* (pp. 162–190). Cambridge: Cambridge University Press.

Braun, M., Scott, J., & Alwin, D. (1994). Economic necessity or self-actualization? Attitudes toward women's labour-force participation in East and West Germany. *European Sociological Review, 10*(1), 29–47.

Chapple, A. (2017). "The Trabant turns 60." *Radio Free Europe.* November 3. Accessed on January 26, 2021 from https://www.rferl.org/a/trabant-car-turns-sixty/28829496.html

Cichanowicz, L. (2016). "GDR brands that have survived capitalism." *The Culture Trip* blog. Accessed April 2, 2019 from https://theculturetrip.com/europe/germany/articles/gdr-brands-that-have-survived-capitalism/

Connolly, K., & Gunther, U. (2002). "Worldwide: Cold War ends as Coca-Cola enters Berlin." *The Telegraph.* Accessed April 2, 2019 from https://www.telegraph.co.uk/news/worldnews/europe/germany/1417292/Worldwide-Cold-War-ends-as-Coca-Cola-enters-Berlin.html

Flaherty, S. (1987). "Guide to the Marlboro oral history and documentation project." *Smithsonian Online Virtual Archives.* Washington, DC: Smithsonian Institution. Accessed on January 21, 2026 from https://sova.si.edu/record/NMAH.AC.0198?s=0&n=10&t=C&q=&i=0

Gureev, A. (n.d.). "Russian automobile—Chaika." *To Discover Russia* website. Accessed on January 21, 2021 from https://todiscoverrussia.com/russian-automobile-chaika/

Hachtmann, F. (2009). Promoting consumerism in West Germany during the Cold War. An agency perspective. *Advertising & Society Review, 10*(2). DOI: 10.1353/asr.0.0025.

Hamer, T., & Hamer, M. (2018). "History of the Trabant Classic German automobile." *Liveabout.com* website. Accessed on January 26, 2021 from https://www.liveabout.com/trabant-built-of-plastic-and-socialism-726030

Hauser, E. (2006). "Cornelsen Verlagsholding GmbH & Co." *Encyclopedia.com*. Accessed January 26, 2021 from www.encyclopedia.com/books/politics-and-business-magazines/cornelsen-verlagsholding-gmbh-co

Hupertz, von H. (2008). "Sandmann in East and West: We have to hit the opposing mission." *Frantfurter Allgemeine*. July 12. Accessed on January 21, 2021 from www.faz.net/aktuell/feuilleton/medien/sandmaennchen-in-ost-und-west-wir-muessen-die-gegnerische-sendung-treffen-1743771.html

Kleiner J. (2017). "Sweet dreams are made of this: The Sandman." *The GDR Objectified* website. May 29. Accessed on January 26, 2021 from https://gdrobjectified.wordpress.com/2017/05/29/sweet-dreams-are-made-of-this-the-sandman/

Roppelt, T. (2014) "Special exhibit: Jeans in former East Germany at the Levi Strauss Museum" *Levi-Strauss website*. Accessed April 3, 2019 from www.levistrauss.com/2014/11/11/special-exhibit-jeans-in-former-east-germany-at-the-levi-strauss-museum/

Ruffner, K. C. (2002). The black market in postwar Berlin. *Prologue Magazine*, 34(3). Accessed on January 26, 2021 from www.archives.gov/publications/prologue/2002/fall/berlin-black-market-1.html

Taylor, F. (2008). *The Berlin Wall: A world divided, 1961–1989*. NY: Harper Perennial.

Wallop, H. (2014). "Rubik's cube invention: 40 years and never meant to be a toy." *The Telegraph*. May 19. Accessed on January 26, 2021 from https://www.telegraph.co.uk/technology/google/10840482/Rubiks-cube-invention-40-years-old-and-never-meant-to-be-a-toy.html

Wiedemann, I. (2003). *Survival strategies of East German companies in a competitive market after reunification*. Norderstet: Diplomarbeiten Agentur Verlag.

CHAPTER 9

Tourism and Mobility in the Eastern Bloc

Michael A. Di Giovine, Ph.D.

A central theme in this exhibition is that walls divide (see Rodden's commentary, Chapter 21, this book). Indeed, our model of the Berlin Wall literally bisects a gallery space that students regularly cross through as they move between classrooms, impeding their normal routines and creating a sense of mild claustrophobia, frustration, and a lack of freedom. The historic Berlin Wall, like all walls, was built to impede mobility, to prohibit the unfettered movement of people and goods from one geo-political space to another. Yet this does not mean that mobility did not exist, nor that the movement of people, goods, and ideas were necessarily and undeniably constrained in East Germany. Likewise, it also does not mean that tourism and leisure travel was not governmentally sanctioned. Rather, the Eastern bloc—and especially East Germany, which was at the frontline of the Cold War—utilized tourism for diplomatic, socio-cultural, and economic reasons—such that the so-called Iron Curtain, as represented materially by the Berlin Wall, could be considered a "semipermeable membrane" (Pedersen & Noack 2019, p. 3; Rosenbaum, 2015). That is, on the one hand, individuals from the West could often enter in (though at varying periods of time only select Easterners could go out), bringing with them not only tourist dollars, but new and different ideas, goods, and preferences. But on the other hand, it also means that tourism and cultural exchange were state sanctioned and promoted between Soviet satellite countries for several reasons explored in our exhibition. Two exhibits in *Faces of the Berlin Wall* focus on the

74 CHAPTER 9 Tourism and Mobility in the Eastern Bloc

Fig. 9.1: Tourism and Mobility in the East

Fig. 9.2: *Postcard Vacations* exhibit

importance of tourism: one at the east side of our wall, designed by student co-curator Aaron Gallant; the other a stand-alone temporary exhibit called *Postcard Vacations*, guest curated by Bulgarian anthropologist Dr. Rossitza Ohridska-Olson in the Francis Harvey Green Library.

The literature defines tourism in several different ways, in part because of differing disciplinary foci: the dominant business and hospitality departments often focus on the mechanics and economics of this particular form of travel, while social scientists like anthropologists, sociologists, and geographers typically concentrate on the socio-cultural effects of hosts, guests, and other stakeholders on each other. Yet most definitions view tourism as a voluntary and temporary engagement with a place that is out-of-the-everyday (geographically and/or conceptually) (Di Giovine 2009a; Urry, 1999). Indeed, as Picard and Di Giovine argue (2013), tourism is predicated on engagement with "Otherness"—again, both physically and conceptually defined. That is, individuals voluntarily use their leisure time to engage in often challenging or taxing voyages away from home to change one's pace, to temporarily step out of the mundane, to experience something different, and even to play out fantasies of being someone else or in some other time and space (Picard & Di Giovine, 2013, pp. 1–23). And while early tourism scholars rightly argued that tourism may perpetuate colonial inequities (Nash, 1977) or privilege superficial, staged experiences (Di Giovine, 2021; MacCannell, 1976), newer generations of scholars have nevertheless perceived of the positive benefits of tourism as a transformative learning experience for self and society (Bruner 1991; Sampaio, Simoni, & Isnart, 2014), and a means of instituting cosmopolitanism and shared identities (Shepherd, 2018).

The German Democratic Republic (GDR) promoted tourism for these reasons, albeit in a highly orchestrated way. It may seem paradoxical that a regime that was clearly restrictive would promote a form of mobility that is intended to engage with otherness in order to foster change, but there were several forms of transformations that the GDR (and other socialist countries, including the Soviet Union itself) needed to foster. The GDR, as a frontline satellite, however, needed to tread delicately, and thus authorized forms of tourism became a central means of exercising control over inevitable social transformation.

On the one hand, the nascent GDR embraced tourism early on as a means of de-Nazifying, yet simultaneously de-Westernizing, the population. That is, tourism was intended as a means of inculcating anti-fascist and anti-capitalistic sentiment by co-opting a common practice that became engrained in the society during early capitalistic and fascist periods. Germans long engaged in leisure travel: During the industrialization period of the late 1800s, urban middle classes would frequently retreat to the countryside to enhance their physical and emotional well-being (Lekan, 2003; Rollins, 1997). In the early 1900s youth groups would often visit the countryside for out-of-the-classroom education (Williams, 1997); this educational youth travel, which included sleep-away summer camps, was taken up by the Nazis in their "Strength through Joy" program (Baranowski 2007; Moranda, 2006, p. 269). Thus, although the communist party considered mass tourism to be an unproductive distraction for its proletariat (p. 268), it was cognizant of the appeal of tourism and its associations with both Nazism and capitalistic mobility. It had to appeal to Nazi sympathizers who looked upon National Socialism's encouragement of enjoyable travel with nostalgia, while at the same time delicately consider those skeptical of totalitarian regimes which, like the Nazis, nevertheless used tourism to promote nationalist ideology. It also needed to show that communism was attractive and not overbearing, and that the communist nation-state was successful enough to allow for leisure-time activities, too. As a report to Stasi chief Erich Mielke said, it would "act as visible evidence of the superiority of socialism over capitalism" (qtd. Bodie, 2020, p. 418). The government therefore utilized what worked—a system of youth travel and packaged group travel plans for adults. While it was not easy to completely eradicate competing travel programs, especially individual and family travel, it nevertheless gradually squeezed out and made illegal alternative travel clubs, or allied themselves with them, such as the venerable and utopian Friends of Nature organization (Moranda, 2006, pp. 270–272).

Indeed, nature tourism was long a preferred form of travel; the urban ruins of the two world wars only made it more preferable. This might have posed a problem for its socialist tourism planners, with their emphasis on proletariat industrialization and work. However, like the Soviet Union and other Eastern bloc states, the GDR was able to re-inscribe the countryside with new imaginaries, and new narratives—imaginaries that were anti-fascist, that valued labor and productivity, and that connected travelers with their socialist brethren. One prime means was to create authorized youth hostels, which would cost little to stay in and which could provide a means of Stasi surveillance and control. Many of these hostels were converted from pubs and inns, or from fascist-era youth lodgings. The government then developed authorized routes and itineraries that would connect these hostels, taking travelers to historic sites commemorating anti-Nazi uprisings or which celebrated local labor movements and industrial achievement (Moranda, 2006, p. 274). As often happens in touristification or heritagization processes (Di Giovine, 2009b), this also served to repurpose sites from the previous era that had outlived their usefulness, such as coal mines and narrow-gauge railways (Hörz & Richter 2011). As Ohridska-Olson shows in her exhibition, *Postcard Vacations*, these travelers (from both the GDR and elsewhere within the Soviet bloc) had a full itinerary of visiting not only communist monuments honoring labor and farming movements, but also historic towns, archaeological sites, ethnographic museums, and even recreated folk villages (see Figs. 9.3 and 9.4) These carried not only patriotic messages, but were showcasing the "Party's" efforts to protect the tradition and heritage of their countries.

In addition, like other leisure-time activities such as museum-going, which, scholars argue, were intended in the 19th and 20th centuries to "civilize" middle-class populations by imposing subtle social control (Bennett, 1995; Duncan 1995), the GDR often produced travel propaganda that would present tourism as purposeful and educational: "Our joy in hiking is altogether different from an escape into nature," said one tour operator (qtd. Moranda, 2006, pp. 274–275). Lectures on packaged tours were *de rigueur*, and guides would be told to interact meaningfully with locals. When visitors stayed in villages or more urban areas, they were often treated to "high art" productions such as opera, plays, folk performances and, in the 1970s and 1980s, pop concerts that were strictly censored and approved by the party (Gorsuch, 2006; Ohridska-Olson, 2019). This was in line with contemporary practices in the USSR and other Eastern European countries, though, Moranda argues, the GDR found it more difficult to squelch the "wild" tourists

Fig. 9.3: Postcard booklet from Tallinn, the capital of Estonia, which was part of the USSR at the time. The images evoke a range of time periods, from the Viking and Medieval eras to the contemporary Soviet period. *Donated by Rossitza Ohridska-Olson*

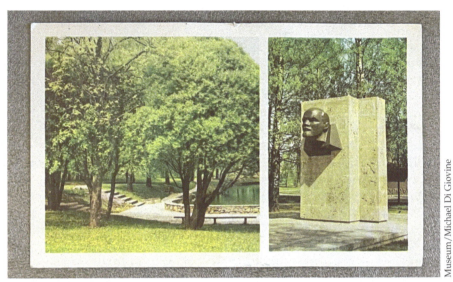

Fig. 9.4: Postcard from Sigulda, Latvia (part of the USSR) featuring a monument to Lenin. The back of the postcard lists the sculptors. *Donated by Rossitza Ohridska-Olson*

Fig. 9.5: Tourist souvenir of a socialist monument. *Donated by Rossitza Ohridska-Olson*

who either argued that the hostels should be open to adults as well, or who remembered earlier versions of freer travel.

Beyond educating the proletariat, the government also recognized the important purpose of leisure travel as a "rite of intensification" (see Graburn, 1977), a break from the work-a-day lifestyle that could refresh and renew the social order. By providing for the needs of workers to rest and recharge their batteries, they could better reproduce the labor power necessary to overcome their capitalist rivals (Bodie, 2020, p. 416; Godau, 1990). It also was used as a carrot to encourage and reward increased productivity (Bodie, 2020, p. 416), just as corporate travel in capitalistic countries do today; thus, these trips—especially expensive ones such as those abroad—were often organized and paid for by the Free German Trade Union Federation (FDGB). As the exhibition, *Postcard Vacations*, shows, this was common throughout the Soviet bloc. The exhibition features a number of postcards from spas, sanatoria, and balneology rest homes that were expropriated from fascist or "bourgeois" capitalists; communist party elites were provided even more luxurious accommodations in palaces and villas. (Interestingly, today these wellness hotels have remained luxury hotels, rather than private residences).

Fig. 9.6: Postcard of a tourist hostel in Ribaritsa, Bulgaria. *Donated by Rossitza Ohridska-Olson*

On the other hand, socialist tourism in the GDR was not only created to remake a nation-state and a population, but it also was undertaken to create a sense of solidarity among other Soviet bloc states. Travel was not simply localized to the domestic realm, but was promoted to other Soviet countries (see Gorsuch, 2011). Although there continues to be a general sentiment that the GDR "walled in" its people, the percentage of East German travelers who traveled abroad was roughly equal to those from France and other European destinations (qtd. in Bodie 2020; qd. in Hill 1993, p. 223; Spode, 1996, p. 14; Studienkreis, 1992). Destinations included the Socialist bloc of Eastern Europe—particularly Poland, Czechoslovakia, and Hungary (Vaizey, 2014), but also father-away countries such as Cuba, where, between 1961 and 1989, tens of thousands of GDR citizens traveled on union-owned cruise ships (Bodie, 2020). Those whose requests for international travel were granted even received a travel stipend from the state.

Why did the communist state, which was so concerned about losing its citizens, pay for them to go abroad? As researchers have shown, the USSR and its satellites used tourism to foster a sense of socialist social solidarity (Hornsby, 2019), a new "proletarian spatial imaginary" (Koenker, 2013). This was particularly important for the central European GDR, argues Görlich, whose citizens

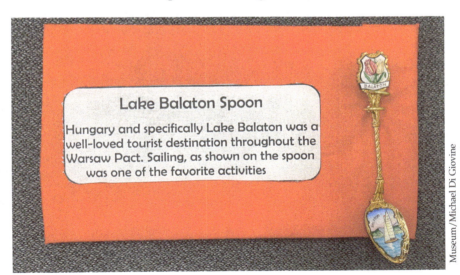

Fig. 9.7: Souvenir spoon from Lake Balatan, Hungary, a popular destination for East German tourists.

were most familiar with the blockbuster sites of Europe that were the historical product of centuries of pilgrimage and leisure travel: France, Spain, Italy, Greece. Thus, in fostering travel within the Soviet East, the GDR attempted to create new mental maps (Lacan [1949] 1977) and imaginaries of what constituted a true tourist destination, and it did not include Paris or Venice or Athens (yet!). In addition, it also was meant to foster an air of friendship between states which, in the recent past, had sometimes fought against each other. But most importantly, it was meant to be "an objective process in which the people of similarly structured socialist societies would increasingly cohere," where the individual state would recede in travelers' mind, fostering a utopian sense of "post-national, unified [socialist] humanity" (Bodie, 2020, p. 415).

Lest it seem that GDR tourism was only outbound—that is, that the government only sponsored their citizens to travel—we must remember, as *Postcard Vacations* makes clear, that travel inside the

Fig. 9.8: Moscow 1980 Olympics postcards. Travel to the birthplace of the revolution was important and supported in the GDR through class trips. This pack of postcards encouraged tourists to participate as they toured in-between the games by taking photos themselves. *Donated by Rossitza Ohridska-Olson*

Iron Curtain went both ways. Indeed, the Soviet Union, which applied an often-heavy hand on the policies of its satellites, were keen to promote tourism for these utopian ends. But it also would specifically send its citizens to the colonies for another purpose: to engage with a socialist Otherness not only in space, but also in time. As Gorsuch argues, Soviet travel accounts of the late 1960s onward presented Eastern Europe as a "younger and less advanced version of the Soviet self," as if they were "going back in time to visit an imaginary, younger, historical Self—an imagining that was used to help justify Soviet domination over the socialist periphery" (2006, p. 207). However, she also argues, their actual experience in the GDR, or Czechoslovakia or Hungary challenged this perspective; they soon realized that "these 'colonies' were in fact more developed than the center" (p. 207).

Similarly, Western tourists (particularly from Nordic countries or West Berlin) were not dissuaded from traveling into the GDR. As Pedersen and Noack argue, "tourism mattered to the socialist bloc's balance of payments and substantiated official claims to 'peaceful coexistence'", and also was a form of soft diplomacy and a bargaining chip for international treaties (2019, p. 2). Western tourists were carefully managed and surveilled, and were shown

Fig. 9.9: Soviet guidebook to East Berlin. *Donated by Rossitza Ohridska-Olson*

Fig. 9.10: Soviet postcard of the Brandenburg Gate, Berlin. *Donated by Rossitza Ohridska-Olson*

the same celebratory socialist sites as domestic tourists; this created competition for scarce resources that often privileged the Western visitor, as they had a much higher purchasing power. While the socialist tourism administration consistently would struggle to keep locals and Westerners apart (Ghodsee, 2005, pp. 92–98), they would nevertheless feature guides who would attempt to demonstrate the benefits of socialism. However, as Standley (2019) argues in her study of East Berlin bus tours, Western travelers—especially day-trippers from West Berlin—would either ignore or aggressively contest their guides' claims. If perceptions did not change, then, would Western tourists at least provide significant income to the state? This, Pedersen and Noack state, is not clear. Tourism, as De Kadt (1979) argued in a UNESCO report, is notorious for economically fostering vertical integration—that is, tourist money is often captured by one organization and does not have the trickle-down effect into local economies as promised (see also Di Giovine, 2009b). Although the Soviet Union ultimately dictated policies to its peripheral satellites, different countries also managed tourism slightly differently. Smaller and less-developed countries such as Bulgaria largely allowed its authorized travel agencies to partner with Western companies for nonpolitical, cheap sun-sand-and-surf vacations, and seemed to economically fare better; in most other countries, tourism was not an economic generator and was made subordinate to more political entities (Pedersen & Noack 2019, p. 11).

Although in the past the study of tourism has been seen as superficial (Leite & Graburn, 2009), an examination of tourism—one of the world's largest and continually fastest-growing industries—is integral for understanding the complexities of the Cold War, as well as the purpose and efficacy of the Berlin Wall. It complicates the understanding that citizens of the GDR were mobility-constrained, or that the East German proletariat worked *in continuum*. It also challenges the idea that disengagement from the dominant capitalistic marketplace fostered a sense of isolation, or of a lack of exchange or cosmopolitan worldmaking. Rather, tourism mattered. It provided a sense of legitimacy and continuity for a nascent communist regime eager to throw off the yolk of fascism and dominance of

Fig. 9.11: Postcard showing the good life at the Bulgarian seaside resort of Primorsko, site of an international youth camp. *Donated by Rossitza Ohridska-Olson*

capitalism. It was a means of socialization, education and indoctrination. And it was a means of world-making: a tool to construct a sense of shared heritage and shared practices among a large swath of land. Much of this was aspirational, but it nevertheless had material consequences. As Koenker states in her now-classic study of Soviet travel, "The history of tourism and vacations is a story of the system and society that the original communists aspired to build, how they envisioned and implemented that society, and how people lived their lives under socialism" (2013, p. 2).

Bibliography

Baranowski, S. (2007). *Strength through joy: Consumerism and mass tourism in the third Reich*. Cambridge: Cambridge University Press.

Bennett, T. (1995). *The birth of the museum*. London: Routledge.

Bodie, G. (2020). 'It is a shame we are not neighbours': GDR tourist cruises to Cuba, 1961-89. *Journal of Contemporary History, 55*(2), 411–434.

Bruner, E. M. (1991). Transformation of the self in tourism. *Annals of Tourism Research, 18*(2), 238–250.

De Kadt, E. l. (1979). *Tourism: Passport to development?* Oxford: Oxford University Press.

Di Giovine, M. A. (2009a). *The heritage-scape: UNESCO, world heritage and tourism*. Lanham: Lexington Books.

Di Giovine, M. A. (2009b). Revitalization and counter-revitalization: Tourism, heritage and the *lantern festival* as catalysts for regeneration in Hoi An, Vietnam. *Journal of Policy Research in Tourism, Leisure and Events, 1*(3), 208–230.

Di Giovine, M. A. (2021). Between tourism and anti-tourism: The ethical implications of study abroad. In John Bodinger de Uriarte & Michael A. Di Giovine (eds.). *Study abroad and the quest for an anti-tourism experience* (pp. 281–324). Lanham: Lexington Books.

Duncan, C. (1995). *Civilizing rituals: Inside public art museums*. London: Routledge

Ghodsee, K. (2005). *The Red Riviera: Gender, tourism, and postsocialism on the Black Sea*. Durham: Duke University Press, pp. 92–98.

Godau, A. (1990). Der DDR-Tourismus nach der Umgestaltung. In F. Stadtfeld (ed.). *Tourismus in einem neuen Europa*. Worms: Fachhochschule Worms.

Gorsuch, A. (2006). Time traveler: Soviet tourists to Eastern Europe. In Anne E. Gorsuch & Diane P. Koenker (eds.). *Turizm: The Russian and East European tourist under capitalism and socialism*. Ithaca: Cornell University Press, pp. 205–226.

Gorsuch, A. E. (2011). *All This is Your World: Soviet Tourism at Home and Abroad after Stalin*. Oxford: Oxford University Press.

Graburn, N. (1977). Tourism: The sacred journey. In Valene Smith (ed.). *Hosts and guests* (pp. 21–36.). Philadelphia: University of Pennsylvania Press.

Hill, R. (1993). Tourism in Germany. In W. Pompl & P. Lavery, (eds.). *Tourism in Europe: Structures and development*. Wallingford: CABI.

Hornsby, R. (2019). Strengthening friendship and fraternal solidarity: Soviet youth tourism to Eastern Europe under Khruschchev and Brezhnev. *Europe-Asia Studies*, 71(7), 1205–1232.

Hörz, P. & Richter, M. (2012). Preserved as technical monuments, run as tourist attractions: Narrow-gauge railways in the German democratic republic. *The Journal of Transport History*, 32(2), 192–213.

Koenker, D. (2013). *Club red: Vacation travel and the Soviet dream*. Ithaca: Cornell University Press.

Lacan, J. ([1949] 1977). The mirror stage as formative of the function of the I. In Écrits: A Selection, trans. Alan Sheridan. NY: W.W. Norton.

Leite, N. & Graburn, N. (2009). Anthropological interventions in tourism studies. In Tazim Jamal & Mike Robinson (eds.). *The SAGE handbook of tourism studies* (pp. 35–64). London: Sage.

Lekan, T. (2003). *Imagining the nation in nature: Landscape preservation and German identity 1885–1945*. Cambridge: Harvard University Press.

MacCannell, D. (1976). *The tourist*. Berkeley: University of California Press.

Moranda, S. (2006). East German nature tourism 1945-1961: In search of a common destination. In Anne E. Gorsuch & Diane P. Koenker (eds.). *Turizm: The Russian and East European tourist under capitalism and socialism* (pp. 266–280). Ithaca: Cornell University Press.

Nash, D. (1977). Tourism as a form of imperialism. In Valene Smith (ed.). *Hosts and guests* (pp. 37–54). Philadelphia: University of Pennsylvania Press.

Ohridska-Olson, R. (2019). *Postcard vacations: The many faces of travel and leisure behind the Berlin Wall*. Exhibition. West Chester University Museum of Anthropology and Archaeology/Francis Harvey Green Library. May 9–Septptember 27, 2019.

Pedersen, S. B. & Noack, C. (2019). Crossing the iron curtain: An introduction. In Sune Bechman Pedersen and Christina Noack (eds.). *Tourism and Travel during the Cold War: Negotiating Tourist Experiences across the Iron Curtain* (pp. 1–20). London: Routledge.

Picard, D. & Di Giovine, M. A. (2013). *Tourism and the power of otherness: Seductions of difference*. Clevedon: Channel View.

Rollins, W. (1997). *A greener vision of home: Cultural politics and environmental reform in the German Heimatschutz movement, 1904–1918*. Ann Arbor: University of Michigan Press.

Rosenbaum, A. (2015). Leisure travel and real existing socialism: New research on tourism in the Soviet Union and Communist Eastern Europe. *Journal of Tourism History*, 7(1–2): 157–176.

Sampaio, S., Simoni, V., & Isnart, C. (2014). Tourism and transformation: Negotiating metaphors, experiencing change. *Journal of Tourism and Cultural Change*, 12(2), 93–101.

Shepherd, R. (2018). *Cosmopolitanism and tourism*. Lanham: Lexington Books.

Spode, H. (1996). Tourismus in der Gesellschaft der DDR. In Hasso Spode (ed.) *Goldstrand und Teutonengrill: Kultur- und Sozialgeschichte des Tourismus in Deutschland 1945 bis 1989*. Berlin: Freie Universität Berlin.

Standley, M. (2019). Experiencing communism, bolstering capitalism: Guided bus tours of 1970s East Berlin. In Sune Bechman Pedersen & Christina Noack (eds.). *Tourism and travel during the Cold War: Negotiating tourist experiences across the iron curtain*. London: Routledge.

Studienkreis für Tourismus (ed.) (1992). Urlaubsreisen 1954–1991. Starnberg.

Urry, J. (1999). *The tourist gaze*. London: Sage.

Vaizey, H. (2014). *Born in the GDR: Living in the shadow of the Wall.* Oxford: Oxford University Press.

Williams, J. A. (1997). Steeling the young body: Official attempts to control youth hiking in Germany, 1923–1938. *Occasional Papers in German Studies, 12*, University of Alberta, June.

CHAPTER 10

Divided Germany, Divided Sports

Jenna Walmer

Jürgen Schult grew up about 35 miles from Schwerin, East Germany. Growing up, he enjoyed roller skating, bicycling, and playing soccer, tennis, and volleyball. Schult won the district championship in cycling, wanted to play soccer, but ultimately he became a world record holder in discus (Janofsky, 1988, p. 1). Ulrich Münch competed in cycling and won the Under-16 East German National Cycling championship in 1985. He made multiple attempts to escape East Germany through Austria-Hungary. These two accounts begin to tell the story of the importance of athletics in East Germany while introducing politicization of athletics due to the division of Germany.

In 1945, the allies divided Germany into East and West. Because of the two different styles of government, life in Germany became drastically different for East Germans and West Germans and the disunion impacted sports. At first, athletics merged for major competitions like the Olympics. As tensions increased, however, so did the debate around unified or divided athletics. Sports became politicized in order to advance each country's motives of division.

Founded in 1948, the German Sport Committee encouraged unity in sports between the East and West. The division of sports started in 1951 when the Socialist Unity Party founded its own Olympic committee (Carr, 1980, p. 41). This started the combination between sports and politics, as it created the divide between East and West athletics. Even with the creation of their own sports committee and Olympic committee, however, German sports were still unified during Olympic Games. The International Olympic Committee demanded the two countries have a joint Olympic committee, and athletes would be chosen from both sides. This debate in 1951 is reflected in the *New York Times*, "The West German Olympic Committee has informed the organizing committee that Germany would take part in the next year's games here (Helsinki). The organizing committee sent its invitation to the West German committee, the only formally recognized German Olympic group, but stressed that it applied to East Germany, too" (Anon, 1951, p. S3). For 1951, it had been decided. The newly divided Germany would continue "unified" in sports, competing together at the 1952 Olympics in Finland.

The next debate arose over the flag representing the joint countries. This issue started when East Germany created a new flag in 1959, adding the communist symbol of a hammer and compass to the traditional German flag (Carr, 1980, p. 47). The decision was made that the two countries would compete under a "neutral" banner, suggested by Avery Brundage, the American president of the International Olympic Committee. The flag's design was "the traditional black, red and gold flag of Germany with five interlocking Olympic rings superimposed on the red bar" (Gruson, 1959, p. 3). This would be the flag used to represent the joint team in future Olympics as well.

Controversy regarding athletics between East and West continued through the proceeding decades. In 1961, West German sports officials severed all sports relations with East Germany in protest against Communist harassment in Berlin. A joint communique from the West German National Olympic Committee and the West German Sports Federation maintained that "henceforth" they would not allow East German athletes to compete in West Germany (Anon, 1961, p. 10). In addition, all West German athletes would boycott all sports events in East Germany. However, the teams competed together for the last time in the 1964 Olympics (Anon, 1963, p. B4). The rising tensions in a unified athletic team reflected the political turmoil.

The division of sports teams was not the only controversy that occurred because of the politicization of sport. Politics also affected the decision to boycott Olympics based on decisions of their allied nations. In 1980, West Germany boycotted the Moscow Summer Olympics, following the United States wishes (Longworth, 1984, p. 5). Later, East Germany struggled to follow the Soviet Union's decision to boycott the Los Angeles games, because of its prominence in athletics. However, they ended up not performing at these games. Overall, athletics and politics coincided with tensions between the two Germanies. Controversies occurred each time a major competition was on the horizon. By 1968, East and West Germany competed separately, allowing East Germany to boast its prowess in athletics (Janofsky, 1989, p. D25).

East Germany was proud of her athletics. Sports became a symbol of superiority and were a national obsession in East Germany. Special schools and programs recruited grade-school children who showed athletic promise. To East Germany, sports were more than just games. Athletics were East Germany's claim to fame. In East Germany, athletics and academics went hand in hand. Young East Germans who showed potential in athletics would be recruited to particular schools that focused on developing athletics. Upon entering athletic schools, children take tests to measure lung capacity, blood oxygen content, musculature and stamina. Students attend classes for 4 hours a day, 6 days a week. Then, they spend up to six hours a day training. The parents only pay 35 marks a month for enrollment in prestigious athletic development schools. Michael Janofsky (1988), writer for *The New York Times*, describes East German athletics as "organized, scientific, and highly efficient" (p. 1). Leipzig was the center of sports. This city had the ninth largest stadium in the world and housed the German Physical Training College (Daley, 1959, p. 20). East Germany produced many top athletes. They competed equally against Finn and Norwegian ski jumpers. Gustav Shur became the world amateur bike racing champion. East German became a powerhouse in athletics through the schools that focused on athletics.

Statistics exemplify East Germany's emphasis on sports. By 1972, East Germany achieved second place in Winter Olympic medal

Fig. 10.1: Uli Meunch's Olympic cycling jersey

count, second to the Soviet Union. In 1984, East Germans won more gold medals than any other country. In the Summer Olympic medal count, they placed third in medal count. In the 1976 Summer Olympics, their female swimmers secured 11 out of the 12 gold medals available (Hersh, 1986, p. 4). The numbers prove the astonishing success of East German athletes, hailing from a country of 17 million.

Overall, athletics in East Germany allowed for legitimacy in the international arena. It took the focus away from the political tensions with West Germany. But in the years following unification, East German athletes and coaches moved to the West. Discussion arose of hosting the Olympics in a once divided country. Some coaches found themselves coaching for a country that no longer existed. By the 1992 Olympics, Germany competed as one nation again (Hersh, 1990, p. 1). Athletics epitomized and followed the rise and fall of tensions in post-war Europe.

Fig. 10.2: Sports medals from the GDR. *Donated by Bruno von Lutz*

Bibliography

Anon. (1951). "Germany in '52 Olympics." *New York Times*. July 15.

Anon. (1961). "Sports Ties Ended: West German athletes told not to compete with East." *New York Times*. August 17.

Anon. (1963). "East, West Germany to join in '64 Olympics." *Chicago Tribune*. March 10.

Carr, G. A. (1980). The involvement of politics in the sporting relationships of East and West Germany, 1945–1972. *Journal of Sport History, 7*(1), 40–51.

Daley, R. (1959). Curtain stays down: Contest between East and West German athletes take place infrequently. *The New York Times*. August 4.

Gruson, S. (1959). "A German flag set for Olympics." *New York Times*. December 7: 3.

Hersh, P. (1986). "East German sports: A mix of success, secrecy." *Chicago Tribune*. May 4.

Hersh, P. (1990). "German sports are in confusing state of disunity." *Chicago Tribune*. September 30.

Janofsky, M. (1988). "East German sports system: The state goes for the gold." *New York Times*. July 3. Accessed from https://www.nytimes.com/1988/07/03/world/east-german-sports-system-the-state-goes-for-the-gold.html on July 9, 2021.

Janofsky, M. (1989). "Athletes ride East German wave." *New York Times*. November 16.

Longworth, R. C. (1984). "Olympics are no game to proud East Germans." *Chicago Tribune*. May 10.

CHAPTER 11

Through Their Eyes

Margaret Hartnett

This exhibit provides a view of the day-to-day lives of people east and west of the Berlin Wall. History looks very different to those living it than as presented in Western textbooks. This exhibit attempts both to challenge people's preconceived notions of what life was like as a German while the wall was up, as well as to convey just how recently such a watershed historical event occurred. This is done by highlighting four people's lived experiences: two from the East and two from the West. Each story is very different, but together they provide a very full picture of what life was like for regular citizens. In conjunction with the corresponding cases displaying typical household artifacts from East and West Germany, *Through Their Eyes* gives viewers a real sense of what life was like; it is built around oral histories collected by the Museum, and displays toys, clothing, media, official documents, and even a piece of the wall. This combination of stories and artifacts allows viewers to put themselves in the shoes of German citizens, from growing up under the presence of the wall to how they remember the wall as adults. Each informant personifies a different theme: With his tale of defection, Uli Meunch embodies the Western myth of the East German who was desperate to leave, while Ivonne Finnin shows that not all Eastern citizens were as oppressed and wall-hating as Western textbooks might depict. Kordula Segler-Stahl's story emphasizes the idea that there were people in the West who were aware of the wall, but that it was not an all-encompassing part of their lives or identity, while Barbara Springer's story illustrates how a simple move could change the entire course of someone's life during this time.

Contributed by Margaret Hartnett. © Kendall Hunt Publishing Company

Eliciting Oral Histories

The history of the wall is complex. Lived experiences on the East and the West varied greatly from person to person. Gathering stories of how multiple people lived helped to inform and inspire this exhibit. Oral histories are much different to work with than traditional, archivally sourced histories (see, for example, Ritchie, 2015; Thompson & Bornat, 2017). When listening to and working with interviews it is important to keep several things in mind, including memory failure and bias (DeBlasio, 2009). When working with Uli, Ivonne, Kordula, and Barbara's interviews, careful consideration of when to convey factual information and when to emphasize memory had to be taken.

Several books written on the experiences of those living near the wall show how there were people on the East who were desperate to leave and that their memories of the wall were filled with pain, while there were also people who looked back on the East as "the good old days" (Funder, 2011). One study found that those who had positive memories relied more on sensory imagery while those who felt more negatively relied on historical records. Likewise, those with positive memories attached their identities more closely to the wall than those who had negative impressions of the wall. The study suggested that emotions pertaining to the wall had a great effect on the way their experiences were remembered and relayed (Bohn & Berntsen, 2007). This corresponded with our oral history elicitations as well. When talking about the wall and their childhood, Ivonne and Barbara discussed personal memories about their upbringing, while Uli and Kordula provided more factual data about the wall in their discussions.

What is interesting about these four accounts is that, despite very different upbringings and experiences, we can find common historical and cultural threads. In some ways, they reveal that people went about their day-to-day lives largely irrespective of the wall's presence. All felt a sense of German pride, even if some, such as Kordula, mused that they would have been better off as two separate countries. Another commonality is that, whether raised in the Soviet-influenced East or American-influenced West, all four moved to the United States at some point. Could their experiences with the wall have led them to crave a society different than their own? The goal of this exhibit is to show similarities—the humanity—among people on both sides of the wall and the people viewing the exhibit.

Thomas Marcus Hans Ulrich (Uli) Meunch

The story of Uli Meunch demonstrates the desperation to leave East Germany that some citizens—even those relatively privileged ones—felt.

Uli was born in 1969 in Halle, East Germany (GDR). Growing up in the GDR, he was heavily involved in sports, especially cycling. He even went to a special school in East Germany that focused on sports. In 1985, when he was teenager, Uli won the national under-16 championship for cycling. Subsequently, he joined the 1988 Olympic trials but didn't make it to the games. His love of cycling was a major influencer of his decisions throughout his life and his ability to leave East Germany.

Looking back on his childhood, he remembers that, in school, things became more overtly political as he got older. Like most other East German children, he remembers being a part of the Thalmann Pioneers—the equivalent of the Boy and Girl Scouts. He remembers when the wall went up, families living on both sides were separated; in his own family, some of his aunts and uncles were on one side and some were on the other side. The wall, to young Uli, was simply a "fact of life" (interview, 4/12/19). He recalled that most homes didn't have a telephone, so the separation seemed even greater; citizens would have to apply to the government to make a call, and when the call would go through, you could hear a "click" as a government representative would listen in. An independent thinker, Uli had a hard time grasping the restrictions he was placed under as a child, but understood it more as he got older. He remembers feeling that the divisions were very unnatural; this was reinforced by the many critiques of the government and the wall that were said behind closed doors.

When he was 19, he graduated from high school and went to Hungary on vacation, with the intent of an escape. A popular vacation venue for those in the Eastern bloc, Hungary was Uli's "little paradise" not because of its countryside or climate, but because the government was known to be more open to trade and dealings with the West. Like most East Germans, he drove a Trabant—a car that became an icon of East German communism (particularly for Westerners), since although it was produced in the GDR, it would take years to get one (Hamer & Hamer, 2018; Lamensch, 2016). "You could order a vehicle, and 10 to 12 years later you could pick it up!" Uli remembered. "Everyone in the family was registered to buy a car [as soon as you turned 18]. Even if you didn't have the money to buy one you could sell that order" (interview, 4/12/19). His license, as well as a toy Trabant, are displayed in this exhibit.

Those, like Uli, who were dissatisfied with East Germany, could apply to the state to leave. However, this came with grave consequences: they were not only blacklisted, but would have to wait extremely long periods of time to receive an answer. As a result, many who owned Trabants innovated a special symbol to tell others of their status using Inka cigarettes, a popular brand of East

Fig. 11.1: Memorabilia from Uli's East German childhood. Cycling handbook, license, identity cards, and racing uniform. *On loan from Uli Muensch*

German cigarettes. Since the publication of popular novels by Karl May, Native Americans have been romanticized in German culture, and portrayed as protagonists in "cowboy and Indians" dramas (see, for example, LoPinto, 2008). The communist government embraced this imagery, presenting Incas as anti-capitalist fighters against the West. However, ironically, by the 1980s, Inka cigarettes became used as secret anti-communism code; INKA cartons were placed in the back of East German cars as an acronym for *Immer Noch Keine Ausreise*—"Still no leaving"—a silent protest against the immobility that East Germans faced in the GDR (interview, 4/12/19).

Fig. 11.2: Inka and Apollo cigarettes. The Eastern bloc had their own brands of cigarettes. Produced in East Germany, INKA celebrated the image of the anti-capitalist Native American, while Apollo cigarettes were created in the Soviet Union to celebrate the successful Apollo 11 moon landing in 1969. Even though the Apollo 11 was a victory for the United States in the Cold War "space race", Apollo brands popped up everywhere in Eastern bloc states.

Uli never formally applied, but planned his defection. While on vacation he learned that the Austro-Hungarian border was one of the weakest separating Western and Eastern Europe. He decided to attempt an escape, riding his bicycle through a cornfield on the outskirts of a border town. As he rode, he heard shouts, as guards with dogs pursued him until he couldn't ignore them anymore. He was captured, and brought to the town's police station to be interrogate. The interrogation lasted for hours; Uli denied his true intentions the whole time: Why would he want to escape? He's an East German cycling champion; he was out training and got lost. The guards didn't buy it. They kept trying to have him sign a statement, which he refused—after all, it was in Hungarian, and Uli wasn't sure what it said. But as time drew on, the guards were eager to get home to their supper, and eventually dismissed him. He signed a statement but added an addendum saying he wasn't trying to defect. The guards let him go with a warning that if he tried to escape again there would be serious repercussions. He considers himself lucky to have survived that escape attempt; if he had tried to escape in East Germany he would have almost certainly been shot. He was also fortunate that the guards apparently never filed the report to the East Germans, as they were supposed to have done.

Energized, the day after he returned from Hungary, he applied that for a visa to leave again under the pretense of a fake cycling race in Hungary, even faking his invitation papers. Even though it was only a few months later, the situation was already very different (Tagliabue, 1989). This was September 1989—2 months before the Wall would come down. Earlier in April the Hungarian government had turned off their electric fences at the border, and on June 27 the Foreign Affairs Ministers of both countries held a ceremonial fence-cutting ceremony, indicating a step toward the free movement of people between East and West. Indeed, on August 19, less than a month before Uli's second attempt, some nine hundred East Germans on vacation rushed the Austro-Hungarian border during a "friendship picnic" that was being held between the two countries. The East German government was infuriated and took a hardliner approach; Uli wasn't certain he would be let out the GDR.

Uli drove his Trabant to the edge of East Germany, where he gave the border guards his visa, fake cycling invitation and other documents. He was careful not to pack anything, so that he didn't look like he was planning on staying more time than his 2-week bike race. They took his papers, clothes, and car and inspected them for 2 hours before releasing him to go to Hungary. But instead of going to the race, Uli drove his Trabant to the Austro-Hungarian border again. This time, he joined a long line of cars that slowly snaked across the border, past Hungarian police. Noticing his Trabant—the quintessential East German car—a Hungarian border guard pulled him out of line. In very broken German, he questioned Uli.

The border guard asked him only a couple of questions in broken German, one being "are you sure? If you go you do not return, 100%?," then told him he was free to go. That was September 17, 1989. He went on to be helped by the Austrians in getting to West Germany, where he secretly planned to stay with his uncle, though he didn't communicate it with him. When he arrived, he was surprised to find that uncle was already waiting for him. It turns out his uncle had received a telegram from Uli's father, reading "Congratulations on the birth of your new son Uli" and he understood right away that Uli was defecting and planning to stay with him (interview, 4/12/19).

A few months later the wall came down. He does not regret his decision to leave and feels blessed that he was able to achieve his goals in life. Indeed, if Uli had left East Germany just 2 months later than he did his life might have been very different, since he would have been ordered to report for the mandatory draft or face prison. Drafts were issued to men 18 to 50 years old, wherein they had to serve 18 months with the National People's Army (Hummler, 2017). "I was scheduled to go November 2nd, 1989 . . . But by the time I was scheduled to report I was in West Germany, so I got out of that" (interview, 4/12/19). His draft papers are also on display in the exhibit.

Uli's story shows that there were many East Germans that were willing to take great risks to leave the GDR, even those who were relatively privileged. Uli was lucky; many were not. His story also shows how these events did not happen a long time ago, but rather recently. In 2001, he moved to the United States and currently lives in Delaware working for a software company. It is hard to even begin to imagine what he went through just by looking at him. His love of the United States was emphasized in the exhibit through his quote, "[Moving to the US] is like a childhood dream . . . I appreciate the spirit here. Compared to Germany it's a different lifestyle, different demeanor and I enjoyed it a lot more . . . I thought if I ever had the chance to work here or live here for a year or two I would go for it" (interview, 4/12/19).

Ivonne Finnin (Nitsche)

While Uli clearly had been discontent with life on the east side of the wall—to the point of risking his young life to escape—Ivonne had a very different perspective, one of a relatively happy and normal childhood. There were people on the East who did not feel actively oppressed and lived relatively happy and normal lives.

Ivonne was born in 1978 in Tetrow, East Germany—a rural town not far from the Baltic Sea. She comes from a long line of working

Fig. 11.3: Five generations of Nitsche/Finnin women: Ivonne Finnin and family

women. Both her grandmother and mother were born and raised in Germany. Her grandmother, Rita Martha Flagel, was born in 1936 in Berlin and was orphaned at age 15 during World War II. She strongly supported communism, thanks to the help that the party provided her throughout her life. In high school Rita wanted to go to college, but her widowed mother relied on her to work to support the family; the monthly stipends that the government provided were quite paltry. Undeterred, Rita was to the principal of her school, who was also a high-up member of the Communist Party, and told him about her plight. The next month, higher stipends arrived at her home—enough that her family could support Rita's ambition to pursue higher education and become a teacher. Upon graduating teacher's college, the party provided her with a job in the north, where she became a principal herself. Her career ended, however, after the wall went down. She was forced into early retirement, but she reinvented herself, working in the tourism industry. She was finally able to travel to places that previously weren't allowed.

Rita's daughter, Ivonne's mother, was born in 1960 in Tuerkow, Germany. She grew up in East Germany and had the value of hard work impressed on her from her mother. She married at 18, worked as Director of the German Red Cross in Tetrow, and took evening classes at a local school. She also supported the government, feeling like it provided fair opportunities and encouraged people to work hard. They both felt as though there was a lot more community and less divisive competition.

Ivonne does not remember growing up in East Germany as a bad thing. She remembers that childcare was extremely accessible and of high quality. Food was never short in her childhood. Ivonne remembers that there wasn't a lot of choices, but there was always enough to eat. Her family always had a garden and there was very little waste. The main hot meal for students was usually lunch, then dinner at home was something light. Ivonne also received high-quality health care. "Everyone was immunized, so, in many ways, they were kind of progressive in that. Every time you received an immunization it was stamped in here. They just felt it was taking good care of the children" (interview, 4/10/19). Mandatory vaccination started in Germany in 1874 and was strictly enforced in the GDR, as they strove for high vaccination rates (Klein, Schöneberg, & Krause, 2012). Ivonne's immunization is displayed in the exhibit.

Fig. 11.4: Ivonne's East German immunization records and favorite book

Like Uli, Ivonne participated in the Pioneers. Founded in 1946, the organization worked to introduce the ideas of socialism and communism to German youth. The organization held regular meetings and taught socialist ideology and morality through the use of organized activities, celebration days, trips, and more (Anon, 2013). Particularly for the younger children, it was couched in terms of play, and Ivonne has fond memories of the festivals and events that the Pioneers held. Children would rise through the ranks; the photo and Pioneer's uniform on the left were for younger children, and Uli's blue shirt were for the older ones. "I was very proud to receive my first uniform," she reminisces (interview, 4/10/19). Like Uli, she didn't remember the organization as being overtly political, but in retrospect they realize that, as they rose through the ranks, the older they got the more political the Pioneers became. "Every year after school you would have little fun activities . . . I never thought 'oh my God this is so political.' . . . We were told to be ready for peace and socialism" (interview, 4/10/19). Indeed, looking back, she also

Fig. 11.5: Pioneer uniforms. Left: girl's uniform; right: Uli's uniform

remembers feeling bad for the handful of Catholic children in her community, who were left out. Since the Church was strongly anti-Communist, many Catholic parents wouldn't allow their children to participate in the Pioneers. She didn't recognize the political and ideological reasons behind this choice.

Ivonne also has positive feelings about her education, and has kept the books she adored as a child. Many of them, including her favorite book of fables on display in this exhibit, were authored by Russians, presenting Soviet propaganda and educating children on Russian cultural classics such as Tolstoy (see Di Napoli, 1994). "I remember I was so sad when I finished this book and I haven't read it in 30 years . . . I'm sure there is a lot of propaganda in it that I didn't pick up, [but] it was my favorite book" (interview, 4/10/19). But if the government did exercise censorship (see Bradley, 2018), it didn't stand out to her as overt or oppressive. Indeed, she feels that her education was high quality and that it set people up to be successful. However, she did remember learning about World War II and having nightmares about being chased because of the things her ancestors did.

Contrary to some perceptions, Ivonne's community watched Western television, where they consumed images and advertisements of Western toys and products such as Barbie dolls that they couldn't have in the East. "I remember seeing the Barbie dolls that they had in West Germany [while watching West German TV] and I couldn't get one when I was a little kid," she said, "and I remember thinking, 'oh everything must be so nice over there.' But on the other hand we did have school propaganda when we were reading books of homeless people being homeless on the streets [in the West] and we just always thought 'oh my goodness that must be so horrible; yes we don't have the stuff but at least we don't have homeless people living out on the streets in the capitalistic society.' All we had were the Sandmann toys" (interview, 4/10/19). Produced in West Germany but popular in both countries, the Sandmann was the star of a stop-motion TV series from 1959 called Unser Sandmannchen, which was East Germany's response to a West German version of the show called *Gruss for Kinder*. The show ran for over 35 years and was broadcast every night at 6:50. It was bright and colorful and apparently not overtly political. Many of the episodes did have political undertones, but not so much that it was unwatchable. To this day, many Germans comment that the East German version of the Sandmann was preferable to the West German version, and despite not having her Barbie, Ivonne has fond memories of her Sandmann doll (Kleiner, 2017).

Ivonne was 11 years old when the wall came down and the two countries unified. She remembers that when the money changed, East Germans felt that they didn't get enough and the West Germans felt that they gave too much. The first time she was able to go over to West Germany it was completely different than what she expected it to be, as it was not nearly as glamorous as the West German TV ads made it appear, but not as bad as she was made to believe in school.

Ivonne originally planned on coming to the United States for a year, but has now been here for over 20. She married an American and has three children. She jokes that she is a first-generation stay-at-home mom, since her mother and grandmother both worked like most women in East Germany. Indeed, when her grandmother visited, she was concerned that not working would not be as fulfilling.

Ivonne's story exemplifies how the lived experiences in East Germany provide a very different view of history than that given in Western textbooks, which often present a constantly suffering populous. Ivonne certainly not feel that way. She feels like she had a relatively normal childhood and she never felt overtly oppressed by the wall.

Barbara Reichel Springer

Some people, upon sensing the growing tensions at the border, moved from East to West Germany before the wall was officially erected. Barbara's family was one of them. This gave her a unique perspective, as she felt that she had roots on both sides of the wall.

Barbara was born in 1945 in East Germany, where she lived until the age of 4 when her family, upon sensing that something was happening, moved to West Germany to a home only about 100 feet from the wall. She remembered the wall going up and how many

Fig. 11.6: Barbara Springer

people tried and failed to escape. She recalled hearing gunfire at the wall, as well as how often animals like rabbits and dogs would trigger the guards at the death strip.

Her passport on display is also a powerful visual reminder of how easily she could have had a different nationality, and different constraints, if it wasn't for her family's decision to move. This passport represents Barbara's mobility in the Western world.

Barbara worked as a seamstress. Like those who practice other trades, Barbara had to complete training in a trade school and receive a *Gesselenbrief*, or a certificate certifying that she can work in that trade. Barbara's *Gesselenbrief* is on display here (Fig. 11.7).

Barbara married a U.S. serviceman in 1965, then moved to the United States. "Dad was a driver for one of the base commanders and would spend his time driving around Berlin. He would see mom riding her bicycle . . . they would talk for a bit, he would ask her out and she would say no." said her son, Jody Springer

Fig. 11.7: Barbara Springer's *Gesselenbrief*

(interview, 4/8/19). Dating a U.S. soldier was not looked upon well by her family, who had lived through World War II and were experiencing the United States' occupation of West Germany. Yet they loved each other, and decided to get married. Their marriage was even more scandalous, since the only way her parents would agree to her marriage to a U.S. soldier was to fake a pregnancy. The couple eventually went on to have two sons. Her time in Germany fostered a life-long love of gardening and canning the things that she grew.

Barbara returned home for a visit in 1968. She was shocked by how quickly the wall had gone up in only a few short years. "They started in overnight, that was so amazing," she commented. "Nobody knew anything, and you get up and there they were working, putting it up." She thought that after a few years of the wall's existence, no one ever thought it would come down. She thought that people just accepted the wall as a part of life in Berlin (interview with Springer family, 4/8/19).

But the wall did come down, and Barbara remembered the mass exodus of Easterners into the West. Many businesses closed in the East, while they thrived in the West. Businesses on the West had a hard time keeping up with the demand for fresh vegetables, as the people coming from the East were amazed by the availability of them and bought as much as they could. She described the scene after the fall of the wall as "festive . . . like an extended party." The wall had been such an iconic presence in her life that she felt that she needed to return, to obtain a piece of the wall. Barbara took a small hammer and chisel to the wall but the little hammer broke; she needed to go back with a bigger hammer. She found a section of the wall graffitied in pink, blue, and orange (interview with Springer family, 4/8/19).

"I had to have one with some color on it," she mused. She chipped them off and brought them to America, where her local newspaper wrote a story about her experience in West Germany and her need to preserve a tiny piece of the wall. That newspaper and multicolored piece of the wall are on display in the exhibit, providing a powerful view of Barbara's optimism and understanding of the events she lived through.

Fig. 11.8: Returning for a piece of the wall. A piece of the Berlin Wall chipped off by Barbara, along with her passport and a newspaper article recounting the event.

Kordula Segler-Stahl

Unlike Barbara, Kordula was from the West—born and bred. Kordula was born in 1952 in Braunschweig, West Germany to a north German mother and a father whose family had fled the Soviet East shortly after World War II. Kordula was very much aware of the wall, but it was not something that defined her life. She studied biology in Stuttgart, and earned a Ph.D. in zoology.

She remembers her childhood as being very wholesome and idyllic, with a lot of "controlled freedom." She doesn't remember any time that her family lacked access to products they wanted, and they always had enough to eat. She enjoyed school and continued her studies in biology in Stuttgart, eventually earning a Ph.D. in zoology. Her mother adored John F. Kennedy, and although she didn't pay much attention when he visited Berlin when she was 13, she knew her was strongly admired by West Germans. However, she was quick to mention that although Americans give Reagan credit for the countries' reunification, Germans today feel that Soviet premier Mikhail Gorbachev and his policies were really responsible for the fall of the wall (interview, 4/5/2019).

East Germany was not a big deal to her a child. She didn't really know anyone there and her understanding of it as a child was that it was a place to which you couldn't go, even though she had one very elderly relative who lived there to whom they would send care packages. She also knew that her mother had friends in East Germany to whom she would write, although no one knew if those letters were actually received.

She was 10 years old when she first glimpsed the wall. Her father took her to Berlin to see a memorial to someone in her family, whom she did not know, who had died attempting to cross over the wall. She later went back and forth between East and West Germany several times, especially when she was a student, because West Germans were free to cross the border.

"I remember as a student traveling to Berlin using that transit Autobahn . . . we had a tote bag full of West German magazines that we would leave at the rest areas." Leaving *STERN* and other West German magazines may have been Kordula's way of peacefully protesting East German censorship (Augustyn, 2017). Yet in crossing the border, she thought that being checked so thoroughly at the checkpoints felt very dehumanizing and that East Berlin was very depressing. She was always relieved to go back to her home in West Germany. She and her friends felt that they were the lucky ones since they weren't trapped.

Kordula lived in the American sector of Germany and later the French sector. There was a strong anti-American sentiment in the American sector through much of Kordula's time there, mostly related to the Vietnam War and the desire to place missiles in Germany pointed at Moscow. The 1970s was marked by a good deal of leftist terrorism and kidnapping in Europe, which led to Americans becoming targets for violence in Germany. One of those terrorists looked like Kordula, which meant that she had to convince the border guards that she was who she said she was every time she crossed back into the West. Nevertheless, Kordula

Fig. 11.9: Artifacts reminiscent of Kordula's youth in West Germany

remembers interacting with the American and French soldiers in the bars and pubs in West Germany, as represented by the Dortmunder Bier bottle and a beer stein.

Kordula was living in Brussels, Belgium when the wall fell. She remembers being glad that people were finally free. But like a significant number of Westerners, she thought that it would have been fine to keep Germany as two separate countries, since she felt that their cultures and financial issues were quite different. Indeed, she continues to perceive marked differences between West Germans and East Germans, even after the fall of the wall. She feels that West Germans had a lot more self-confidence and were a lot more outgoing, while East Germans appear more suspicious and see Westers as boastful and overpowering. After reunification, she visited the East, where she taught workshops for an American company; she noticed that people were very withdrawn, which she feels is a residual effect of their lives before the wall fell.

Even today, she feels that she wouldn't want to live in the East because of the strong German nationalism there. She is currently retired and lives in West Chester.

Traditional Western textbooks make it seem as though everyone in both East and West Germany was constantly consumed by the wall and that when it came down all differences disappeared in a united Germany. Kordula's story shows that that was not necessarily the case. She shows a side of history where people were able to lead normal lives alongside the wall. The wall has fallen, but the barriers remain.

Bibliography

Anon. (2013). "German democratic republic: Youth movement." *Historic Clothing* website. February 20. Accessed April 2019. https://www.histclo.com/youth/youth/org/pio/pioneerg.htm

Augustyn, A. & Editors. (2017). "Stern: German News Magazine." *Encyclopædia Britannica*. September 06, 2017. Accessed April 2019. https://www.britannica.com/topic/Stern-German-news-magazine

Bohn, A. & Berntsen, D. (2007). Pleasantness bias in flashbulb memories: Positive and negative flashbulb memories of the fall of the Berlin Wall among East and West Germans. *Memory & Cognition*, 35(3), 565–77.

Bradley, L. (2018). "The secret of East German censorship." *Who's Watching Who?* Blog November. Accessed April 2019. https://www.blogs.hss.ed.ac.uk/whos-watching-who/tales-archive/secrets-of-east-german-censorship/

DeBlasio, D. M. (2009). *Catching stories: A practical guide to oral history*. Athens, Ohio: Swallow Press, 2009.

Di Napoli, T. (1984). Thirty years of children's literature in the German democratic republic. *German Studies Review*, 7(2), 281–300.

Fisher, A. (2015). Reliving the Berlin Wall days. *Reason*, 47(5), 62.

Funder, A. *Stasiland*. Victoria: Penguin Random House Australia.

Hamer, T. & Hamer, M. (2018). "History of the trabant classic German automobile." *Liveabout.com* website. Accessed on January 26, 2021 from https://www.liveabout.com/trabant-built-of-plastic-and-socialism-726030

Hummler, R. (2017). "War resisters' International." *Country Report and Updates: Germany*. October 1. https://www.wri-irg.org/en/programmes/world_survey/country_report/de/Germany

Klein, S., Schöneberg, I., &Krause, G. (2012). "The historical development of immunization in Germany. From compulsory smallpox vaccination to a National Action Plan on immunization." National Institutes of Health. *Bundesgesundheitsblatt, Gesundheitsforschung, Gesundheitsschutz*. November 2012. Accessed April 2019. https://www.ncbi.nlm.nih.gov/pubmed/23114451

Kleiner, J. P. (2017). "Sweet dreams are made of this: The Sandman." *The GDR Objectified* blog. May 28. Accessed April 2019. https://gdrobjectified.wordpress.com/2017/05/29/sweet-dreams-are-made-of-this-the-sandman/

Knabe, H. (2019). "Hubertus Knabe." *TED* talk. Accessed April 7, 2019. https://www.ted.com/speakers/hubertus_knabe

Lamensch, G. (2016). "Not the only car in town: The East German automotive industry beyond the trabant." *CENTRALBERLIN* Blog. June 17. Accessed April 23, 2019. https://www.centralberlin.de/blog/not-the-only-car-in-town-the-east-german-automotive-industry-beyond-the-trabant/

Lathan, S. R. (2014). A medical student trapped behind the Berlin Wall, 1961. *Baylor University Medical Center Proceedings, 27*(1), 66.

LoPinto, N. (2008). Der Indianer. *AlbertaViews*. July 1. Accessed on April 9, 2021 from https://albertaviews.ca/der-indianer/

Ritchie, D. A. (2015). *Doing oral history*, 3rd ed. Oxford Oral History Series.Tagliabue, J. (1989). "Even more East Germans may now leave for West." *The New York Times*. November 5. Accessed April 1, 2019. https://www.nytimes.com/1989/11/05/world/even-more-east-germans-may-now-leave-for-west.html

Thompson, P., & Bornat, J. (2017). *The voice of the past : Oral history*. Oxford: Oxford Oral History Series.

CHAPTER 12

Excerpts from
Connections: Memoirs of an American Historian in the Communist East Bloc

Claude Foster; edited by Brenda Gaydosh

Fig. 12.1: Claude Foster

As history professor Claude R. Foster prepared for retirement from West Chester University (1967–2008), he began to write his memoirs. For over three decades, Dr. Foster studied and taught in West

Germany, studied and presented papers in East Germany, and led groups of students throughout the Communist East Bloc. Below are excerpts from his memoirs[1] (Foster, 2019):

> (1964) The time fixed on my visa was about to expire. I had to return to the BRD. Before exiting East Berlin at the Friedrich Straße rail station, I entered a café to have a cup of coffee and some pastry. It was rare to find a table for oneself alone. I noticed a free place at a table where a young woman sat. Approaching the empty chair, I addressed the young woman, "May I sit here?" She nodded consent and said, "Bitte schön." We came into conversation. She noticed my luggage that I placed next to the table and also my camera that I had placed on the table. "Are you an American," she asked. "Yes," I responded. "I am now about to return to the BRD." She sighed, "With your passport, you can walk through that checkpoint into the West, but I can't. The wall separates Germany from Germany and has caused much heartbreak. My husband is in the BRD and I am here with our little daughter. He cannot come to us and we cannot go to him." "How did that happen?" I asked. The young woman was attractive, but her face and eyes revealed a certain sad resignation. She answered, "When the borders were sealed on August 13, 1961, my husband was playing in a dance band in West Berlin. He realized that if he came back to East Berlin he probably never would be able to perform in the West again. A certain period of grace was given for DDR citizens in the BRD to return to the DDR. My husband, hoping to be able to arrange for the emigration of his wife and daughter to West Berlin, remained in West Berlin to work for our emigration. The grace period for his return expired and his efforts to acquire emigration for his family failed. Now he is in West Berlin and his wife and daughter are in East Berlin, and a high wall and armed guards seal our segregation. Of course, we are in contact by mail, but that is no substitute for the personal presence of a husband and a father. Because I have no telephone, and anyway there is no telephone connection between

---

[1] The editor would like to thank the Foster family for permission to reprint these excerpts.

East and West Berlin, our little daughter doesn't even get to hear her daddy's voice." I interjected, "You mean that you have not seen your husband or your daughter her father since August 1961?" The young woman responded, "We meet for three weeks of vacation each summer on the Black Sea in Romania. My husband now has a BRD passport. At the end of those three weeks, it is very difficult for us to part, for it means almost an entire year without any personal contact. The separation is particularly difficult for our little girl."

(1973) On a later visit to Dresden, while returning on the ship that conveyed us from Saxon Switzerland to the center of the city, I noticed a man in long and intense conversation with some members of my group. Of course, in those days, DDR citizens were anxious to have conversations with people from the West. I casually walked past the group in order to discern the theme being discussed. The DDR citizen was probing the Americans to discover details about their stay in the DDR. I recognized immediately that the man was a member of the Stasi, the DDR secret police. On a pretext of calling attention to a castle on the Elbe bank, I interrupted the conversation. I then drew some of the group aside and reminded them of instructions I earlier had given each person. Never mention names of your DDR hosts. Never reveal that you are residing overnight with a family. This last point was important because our residence accommodations were in the Weimar Hospiz, not with a private family in Dresden. Conceivably one could, by taking the earliest train from Weimar to Dresden and the latest train from Dresden to Weimar, spend most of the day in Dresden and still be able to return late to Weimar. We permitted the Stasi agent to believe that this was our plan. Of course, we planned to remain overnight in Dresden where we were hosted by several families. Perhaps the agent suspected that we intended to remain overnight in Dresden, and, after we left the ship, he followed us. He kept a block behind so that we would not notice that we were being trailed. I had to discover a way to shake off this undercover leech. From the pier, we walked toward a main street, Ernst Thälmann Straße. At that intersection, when we turned the corner into Ernst Thälmann Straße, we would be out of sight of our pursuer. At that point, I instructed the group to stop and to look at the books on display in the window of a large bookstore. When the agent turned the corner in hot pursuit, he was startled to see us standing in front of the bookstore. Of course, he could not stop because that would have made his trailing us too obvious. He proceeded slowly down Ernst Thälmann Straße, always looking back to see if we resumed our march. At the corner was a streetcar stop. I saw a streetcar coming. It halted to discharge and take on passengers. At the very last minute before the streetcar doors closed and the trolley proceeded, I hustled my group onto the car. Under full speed, we passed the Stasi agent standing frustrated on the sidewalk. The next stop was too far away for the thwarted stalker to catch up with us. This was a good lesson for naive Americans. The group had not realized that this deputy had been pumping them for information.

(1983) Our last stop was East Berlin. After visiting the historic sites, the Pergamum Museum, the Berlin Dom, the French Huguenot Church, Saint Hedwig's Cathedral, the Brandenburg Gate and a sightseeing boat ride on the River Spree, we took refreshments in the flat of Frau Charlotte Rhode. Now we were prepared to cross over into West Berlin through the check. At the checkpoint, each member of the group surrendered his exit card to the border patrol officer. This card had been issued to us along with the visa that each person had received from the DDR Berlin Travel Bureau and was required to be turned in upon exiting the territory of the DDR. Mrs. Helder could not find her exit card. I had to keep the group together. Everyone had to wait until Mrs. Helder found her exit card. The guard was adamant. We could not leave his post until the exit card had been turned in. We searched through Mrs. Helder's luggage. No card could be found. I noticed that the tension provoked by this situation was causing Mrs. Helder to become very upset. I tried to reason with the guard. "Surely you can understand that an elderly person, who does not speak German and who has spent 3 weeks in the DDR, might have lost the exit card." The guard remained intransigent. I then requested, "May I speak to your senior officer?" The guard went to the office behind the counter. Soon the subordinate returned with his senior officer who was in charge of the checkpoint. "You must return the exit card," the senior officer said, "before you are permitted to cross the border. That's the rule." How often had I heard that word in the DDR!-Vorschrift! (rule).

"But the lady has lost the exit card," I countered. "Tuts mir leid, (I regret,"), the officer replied. Having visions of being forced to remain in the DDR, Mrs. Helder, seated on a bench, began to tremble. Recalling the stress-provoked coronary death of the BRD citizen, Rudolf Burkert, on Sunday, April 10, 1983 at the Berlin/Drewitz border station, and the tension-evoked coronary death of Heinz Moldenhauer on Tuesday, April 26, 1983 at the Wartha/Herleshausen border point, deaths that had caused very bad publicity for the DDR in the international media, I said to the senior officer, "Herr Oberst, you see that elderly lady trembling. She has a heart condition. Permit me to remind you that if this elderly person, because she lacks a simple exit card, should suffer a coronary attack on your watch, you bear full responsibility." The senior officer then said, "She may leave."

That evening in a West Berlin hotel, I lay in bed reading. Mrs. Helder and her daughter shared a room next to mine. There was a knock on my door. I opened the door and there stood Mrs. Helder and her daughter. "We found the exit card," they exclaimed. "What?" I responded. The daughter explained. "Each night before mother goes to sleep, she reads a passage from her Bible. She had placed the exit card as a bookmark in her Bible. We never thought to look in her Bible for the card." We laughed.

(1989) On November 9, 1989, the Berlin Wall was opened. A few days later, I arrived in West Berlin and was astounded to see so many East Berliners and other DDR residents roaming Kurfürstendamm and crowding the shops where they wished to spend their one hundred West German marks welcome money, distributed by West Berlin banks. Because the regular banks were overwhelmed with people waiting for their welcome money, the municipal government stationed trailers (mobile banks) strategically throughout the city to help relieve the pressure. Because of the masses of people, Kurfürstendamm was closed to traffic. More than 300,000 people flooded the center of West Berlin. Despite the serious phenomenon of sudden liberty on display, there was a humorous side to the spectacle. The DDR residents were easy to identify. Most of them had either an orange or a banana in hand. Oranges and bananas were rare in the DDR. Once in West Berlin, the DDR citizens stormed the fruit stands.

The vain gestures at reform that the Politbüro daily made to the DDR population were unable to stem the tide or to silence the increasingly loud chorus for democracy and unification (Freiheit und Einheit). These words were the same revolutionary code words that the student fraternities had invoked in the 1817 Wartburg Congress. What once had been expropriated for DDR propaganda (the student revolutionary activity of 1817) now was turned against the Politbüro. Token reforms and a rearrangement of political furniture inside the Politbüro could not satisfy the masses, and the attempt at reform verified Alexis de Tocqueville's (1805–1859) observation: "The most dangerous moment for a tyrannical regime usually occurs when it seeks to reform itself." The continuous reports of economic and social progress issued by the Politbüro were belied by the obvious economic and material decline in the DDR. After 40 years of residence in the DDR, the population sided with the Roman philosopher, Seneca (4 B.C.–65 A.D.): "People believe their eyes more than their ears."

The S Bahn trams (elevated train) from Friedrich Straße (border point between West and East Berlin) to the Zoological Garden (Zoo) in West Berlin were jammed with travelers. Traveling from Friedrich Straße to Berlin Zoo, the travelers were empty handed, but the return journey from Berlin Zoo to Friedrich Straße, saw each person burdened with packages of every description. Carrying a heavy suitcase, I managed to squeeze onto one of the cars where people were pressed together as sardines in a can. Gerhard waited for me at the Friedrich Straße station and, after passing through border control, which the DDR officials still pretended was necessary, we walked the four blocks to the Johannes Hof.

Because I wanted to be certain that I could retrieve souvenir pieces of the rapidly disappearing wall, one afternoon, after having completed my session with Gerhard in his office, I walked along the wall's perimeter between Potsdamer Platz and the Brandenburg Gate with Charlotte Rhode. Ever since Charlotte hosted my pupils and me in 1967 when, from her balcony, we had viewed the International Communist Youth Parade, each subsequent summer she extended warm hospitality to my group and me. Charlotte and I collected the fragments, which were being chipped out of the body of this massive 28-year-old concrete giant. The sound of hundreds of chisels and picks assaulting the stubborn, reinforced cement echoed along the wall in a never-ending demolition staccato. Charlotte and I were quite content with the pieces we were able to collect.

Bibliography

Foster, C. (2019). *Connections: Memoirs of an American historian in the communist East Bloc.* Edited by Brenda Gaydosh. Grosse Ile, MI: Alpha Academic Press.

CHAPTER 13

Tears in Bitterfeld

Claude Foster

The telegram message,
brief as a Roman dagger,
pierced her heart.

"Klaus killed—
last night in automobile accident.
Can you attend funeral?"

The raised letters on the thin paper,
like a branding iron,
burned a deep wound into her heart.

"Klaus, dear Klaus," she wept,
and sank into her chair
under the burden of grief.

No, she may not attend the funeral.
East Berlin rejects her visa application
for travel to West Germany.

No, his body may not be buried
in the hallowed soil of his socialist Fatherland.

Contributed by Claude Foster. © Kendall Hunt Publishing Company

Three months ago, he had crossed the border illegally.
Did his mother know of his plans?
DDR functionaries suspected she did.

No permission to attend the funeral of a son
who fled the Republic.

No permission for the Republic fugitive
to be interred in the soil of his native land.

Farewell then, dear son,
from within the alienation which estranges Germany
from Germany.
Only in my thoughts may I, your German mother,
accompany her German son to his
narrow, modest house in German soil.

The smoke from the chemical chimneys
hangs low in the cold, leaden, winter sky.

The mother sits before a window,
looking westward through the dull gray.
Silent tears,
the only witness to grief in Bitterfeld.

In a few years, at age sixty-two,
she would have emigrated to her son.

"T'were better had he remained with her," she thought,
"for now more than barbed wire separates us."

CHAPTER 13 Tears in Bitterfeld

"He cannot return to me,
and I cannot go to him.
Only in some transcendent world
which knows no borders
or political ideologies
will I find him again."

She sighs and whispers his name,
and the frigid winter air bears her lament
before an indifferent race.

Production schedules must be met.
A brigade of blue-shirted Free German Youth marches past,
Skis slung over their shoulders.
A baby cries in the adjoining apartment.
No one notices the tears in Bitterfeld.

CHAPTER 14

New Year's Eve, 1989

Dana Cressler

Having a completely different job/mission from my father in the Army—who was stationed in Berlin when the wall was erected—nothing I am writing is or was a secret.

The overwhelming emotions were joy and excitement for the American Soldiers stationed with me in Germany when it was announced that the Soviet Unit peaceably loosened its grip on the other European countries and East Germany was opening the Berlin Wall. This news signaled that the Soviet Union (i.e., the Soviet Empire) was weakening.

I had arrived in Germany in the summer of 1988 as a young army Second Lieutenant assigned to Echo Company, 708th Main Support Battalion, 8th Infantry Division near Mainz Germany. Echo Company was a Missile Maintenance unit with the mission of repairing anti-aircraft and anti-tank weapons systems (i.e., the sighting systems for the TOW and Dragon anti-tank weapons, the M270 Multiple Launch Rocket System [MLRS], and the Vulcan & Chaparral anti-aircraft weapons). During the little more than a year from when I arrived in Germany and the announcement of the Berlin Wall opening, I had been training to defend Germany against the Soviet Union. I had participated in the last large-scale Reforger (Return of Forces to Germany) exercise and had been to multiple U.S. Army live fire exercises in Grafenwohr and Hohenfels, Germany along the East Germany border. These exercises were to demonstrate the U.S. Military's might to the Soviet Union. I had also scouted out where

Contributed by Dana Cressler. © Kendall Hunt Publishing Company my unit would move to in the event that the Soviet Army invaded Western Germany. My unit was to occupy an elementary school in the region of Germany called the Fulda Gap. The running thought or "joke" was that our mission was to be a speed bump for the Soviet Military as they crossed Germany, in hopes to provide enough time for U.S. Military re-enforcements to arrive. None of us really had the expectation that we would survive such an event. So, when it became apparent that the Soviet Union was weakening, there was great joy and excitement.

My wife and I, along with several other lieutenants and their spouses from my unit, traveled to Berlin to celebrate the New Year with the newly reunited Berlin. Although the Berlin Wall was open, the main way to travel between East and West Berlin was still through Check Point Charlie. As a member of the U.S. Military, I was allowed to cross into East Berlin, but I had to wear my U.S. military uniform. Fig. 14.1 is a picture of my wife and me in front of the Brandenburg Gate in East Berlin (I forgot to bring a coat, but I did have long underwear on—it is cold in Berlin in winter!). We went to a 5-star restaurant in East Berlin and had a multiple-course dinner for about $10 for the both of us; this was before the East and West German currency equalized.

Fig. 14.1: Second Lt. Dana Cressler and wife in front of the Brandenburg Gate, East Berlin

There were many people trying to chisel a piece of history off of the Berlin Wall. Sometimes you had to go high on the wall to get the piece you wanted. Fig. 14.2 shows us getting our souvenirs.

CHAPTER 14 New Year's Eve, 1989 **131**

Fig. 14.2: Chipping a piece of the wall, December 1989

On 31 December 1989 (New Year's Eve), we went to the Berlin Wall that was near the Brandenburg Gate (on the West Side). It was very crowded as you can imagine. David Hasselhoff was singing "Looking for Freedom" from a crane's crow's nest wearing a leather jacket with lights. People in the crowd were shooting off bottle rockets and some were trying to hit him. This is a YouTube link to Hasselhoff's performance: https://www.youtube.com/watch?v=0zXiClnK8oE

As you would suspect, there was much celebration going on by both the East and West Germans. It was very peaceful event (we didn't see any criminal acts or violent acts—although there might have been some that we didn't witness) and there seemed to be great joy and hope in the air. Fig.s 14.3 and 14.4 give a sense of how crowded it was. My wife and I went to New York City one time for New Year's Eve. It was similar—that is, so many people that when

Figs. 14.3 & 14.4: New Year's Eve at the wall

Fig. 14.5: Scaling the wall

the crowd shifts, you have no choice but to shift with it and you get the sense that if you tripped and fell that the crowd would crush you to death. My wife and I got on the wall; it was about 12 feet high (see Fig. 14.5). There were plenty of drunk Germans available to help you up the wall and they helped themselves to free butt "gropes" for their services—at least for helping the ladies! From where we were perched on the top of the wall, we could see East Berlin and the Brandenburg Gate (see Fig. 14.6). We didn't spend much time on top of the wall. I don't remember how wide the top was, but it wasn't too wide. And we wanted to get down before a "crowd surge" on top of the wall pushed us off.

It was great being a part of history.

Fig. 14.6: Dana Cressler and wife on the wall

The Afterlife of the Berlin Wall

Chapter 15: Creating "Berlin" and Creating "The Wall"
Bruno von Lutz

Chapter 16: Commemorating the Berlin Wall
Natalie Fenner

Chapter 17: The Commercialization of the Berlin Wall
Foster W. Krupp and Christian Sabree

Chapter 18: The Berlin Wall in Popular Culture
Brianna A. Eldridge

Chapter 19: Concerts at the Berlin Wall
Jim McAllister

Chapter 20: The Persistence of Division
Brittany Siemon

CHAPTER 15

Creating "Berlin" and Creating "the Wall"

Address given at West Chester University

Bruno von Lutz

Director, German-American Institute Saarland, Germany

The Berlin Wall has disappeared—it is now a mere metal line embedded in the streets crisscrossing Berlin; the real thing has gone. Pieces of the wall pop up everywhere; they are distributed all over the world standing in front of museums, public buildings, in parks—there might even be many more miles of wall distributed over the world than were ever built by the GDR. The wall has become an invisible monument. Today you walk through Berlin and can only imagine the wall, whereas you encounter the real thing even in places such as Philadelphia. At least the Great Wall of China is still there, or parts of Hadrian's Wall in Britain, and you can get an impression of the monstrosity of the construction, whereas the Berlin Wall and the political and human monstrosity connected to it can only be accessed through your imagination or through photography and film. The individual pieces of the wall have been separated from the original and have become mere symbols or *pars pro toto* for oppression and human suffering. In this respect, the wall has undergone a gradual shift from a political and ideological building serving a distinct function, and indeed with no other significance but a wall. Yet soon after its construction it became a symbol of suppression, of the fear by the Eastern powers in the Cold War of infiltration by the West and of losing its citizens

Contributed by Bruno von Lutz. © Kendall Hunt Publishing Company to the West, and in the end, the fear of "convergence," which means the gradual approximation of the socialist and capitalist systems.

Interestingly enough, with its disappearance the wall has become a cultural phenomenon. Where has it gone? Well, a large part of it has gone to the Museum of Modern Art in New York: This institution bought a particularly interesting section of the wall, which was painted on by various artists, the first street art in fact. And this section also played an important role in Wim Wenders' 1987 film *Wings of Desire* (*Der Himmel über Berlin*), starring Peter Falk of *Columbo* fame. Pieces of the wall were sold by the GDR in order to make some much-needed money, the last gasp of the GDR so to speak, albeit a capitalist gasp. A German artist, whose work was on that particular section, sued the GDR for selling his art without getting his permission. The GDR countered by saying that this was not art but a defacing of their property—but they sold it nevertheless as art to the MoMa for 500,000 Deutschmarks. So, this is one of the few structures that have achieved greater significance after they were gone.

Fig. 15.1: Student co-curators visiting the Berlin Wall at Philadelphia's German Society with its director Anton "Tony" Michels (center)

Museum/Michael Di Giovine

***

There were four major crises in the history of post-war Germany's division into East and West, into the GDR, the German Democratic Republic; and the *Bundesrepublik Deutschland*, the Federal Republic of Germany. I will say something about the abbreviation "BRD" for Bundesrepublik Deutschland a little bit later.

1. Berlin Airlift 1948/49—70 years ago
2. Uprising on June 17, 1953 (*"Tag der Deutschen Einheit"*/Day of German Unity)
3. Building of the wall: August 13, 1961
4. Fall of the wall: November 9, 1989

You would expect West Germany, or rather, the united Germany, to make this last date its national holiday. Yet the 9th of November is not an easy date in German history: In 1918, the *Reichskanzler*, the Chancellor of the German Empire, announces the resignation of Kaiser Wilhelm—the beginning of the 1st German Republic; on November 9, 1938 the infamous *Kristallnacht* took place. Thus, the National Holiday/*Tag der Deutschen Einheit* is on October 3 (1990), when the GDR officially joined the State of West Germany. In the GDR, October 7 was the "Tag der Republik"/Day of the Republic, for on October 7, 1949 the GDR was founded.

The abbreviation "BRD" was used by East German politicians and not accepted in West Germany, as it was too close to the abbreviation "DDR" (Deutsche Demokratische Republik), which in English is translated to German Democratic Republic (GDR). A controversy about the abbreviation began in the early 1970s when its use was prohibited in some federal states because it was seen as a "communist invention" employed for agitation by its frequent use in the GDR. By avoiding the abbreviation BRD, the West German side wanted to distinguish itself from the use of the abbreviation in the GDR and prevent the West and East German states from being placed on the same level by analogous abbreviations. The Federal Republic of Germany always regarded itself as the only legitimate German state under international law despite all the relaxation in German–German relations. The West Germans wanted to convey that only the government of the Federal Republic of Germany emerged from recognized democratic elections. It claimed the designation "Germany" for the whole of Germany and thus as a representative of itself. Through the continued use of this term, the existence of a German nation—Germany as a whole—was to be kept in the public consciousness in order not to jeopardize the officially declared national goal of reunification. On May 31, 1974, the heads of government of the Federation and the Länder recommended "that the full term 'Federal Republic of Germany' be used in official language."

From June 1974, school textbooks with the abbreviation "BRD" were no longer permitted by the Conference of State Ministers of Culture (*Kultusministerkonferenz*). In school essays in West Berlin, the abbreviation could be marked as an error by the teachers if the subject of Germany had previously been dealt with in class. All of this is very complicated: the ideological implications, the psychological leverage the wall provided to the West within the framework of the Cold War, the strategic advantage of the East due to the fact that Berlin was surrounded by the GDR and thus vulnerable, the reticence of the Western powers to take counter measures, the pleas of the German government to the Western powers for support etc.

So, this is a talk about, first, the history of the GDR and the Berlin Wall, as well as the subsequent political isolation and the self-imposed cultural isolation of the GDR; and, second, the "Wall" as a construct, a narrative, the "Wall" as a tourist attraction, as a political monstrosity-turned-museum piece largely devoid of historical meaning, and about the symbolization and museumification of the wall—and in general about monuments and their function of power and authority in society. I will also talk about the creation of "Berlin" as a symbol and a reference point for the free world. John F. Kennedy's famed phrase "I am a Berliner" might be said to be the most powerful driver for this. This must be rather sketchy and anecdotal, as things were much more complex at the time, politically and ideologically, than can be dealt with in a short 45 minutes.

***

Only 2 months before work on the wall began, Walter Ulbricht, then-leader of the GDR, answered rumors about plans to build a wall. He said, "Nobody has the intention to erect a wall": This was later dubbed the lie of the decade.

Walter Ulbricht, communist agitator—who returned after exile in Paris, Prague and Moscow to become the leader of the GDR—saw himself forced to cordon off the Soviet sector of Berlin with a wall after the so-called "bloodletting" (then the term): too many people fled from the East to the West.

Economic difficulties, particularly supply problems, caused a dramatic increase in the flow of refugees from the GDR; there was in particular an increasing shortage of skilled workers. In West Berlin and the Federal Republic of Germany alone, 4,770 Germans from the GDR applied for emergency admission between the 10th and the 16th of July. Between 5 and 8 August, another 5,009 refugees registered. Nevertheless, the closure of the border and the beginning of the construction of the Berlin Wall in the night of 13 August hit the Federal Government and the Berlin Senate without any warning from the intelligence services, although everyone expected measures from the GDR to curb the flight movements.

Many pictures were taken of the dramatic situation along the border across Berlin, which then was mostly a barbed wire fence. The most iconographic picture is that of a soldier of the "Volksarmee" soldier leaping across the barbed wire with helmet, gun, and uniform.

It might be quite rewarding to look into the culture of photography along the East German border, as at the time it was photography that distributed knowledge of the wall across the world together

Fig. 15.2: Mauerspringer ("Wall Jumper"). Statue of East German soldier Konrad Schumann famously jumping over barbed wire into West Berlin before the Wall was erected.

with an ideological message: In a way, the wall and the re-enforcements along the border of the GDR. But we must be aware of the fact that the Wall was just a very small part of the line separating the two Germanies, about 170 km crisscrossing through Berlin and surrounding the city, were later somehow an ideological God-send for the West; after all the wall and the *Zonengrenze*—the reinforcement along the border—provided a ready image and symbol for the inhuman ideology of the whole Eastern Block and could thus be used for Western indoctrination.

I quote from a speech by Konrad Adenauer, the then Chancellor of West Germany, in the city of Essen, 5 days after the 13th of August[1]: "What has been granted to the peoples of Africa cannot be denied to the people at the heart of Europe in the long run." With these words, he was declaring that the GDR and the USSR were modern-day colonialist powers.

I am not sure whether this was a clever move, as Britain was right in the middle of de-colonization, and this process was not really completely welcomed by Britain. Strangely enough, the development after the fall of the wall had the characteristics of the West colonizing the East: Today, virtually nothing is left of the East and its everyday culture; the only remaining East German item of daily life is the little green man in the street lights signaling to Eastern and Western pedestrians alike that they may safely cross the street. Many university posts were thought by the West German government to be ideologically tainted, especially the jobs in the Humanities, so virtually everyone had to go, replaced by West German professors. The jobs in the local governments were all filled by people from the West, quite often by older politicians who hoped for a revival of their political career. There were five new Federal States, and each new State had a *"Verwaltungshilfe partnerstaat,"* a partner for administrative support from among the Western States. The Western States were supposed to support their partner State in the creation of new structures of public administration and government. This meant that the new States were more or less bound to follow the example of their Verwaltungshilfe partnerstaat. Between 1990 and 1995 roughly 35,000 West German civil servants were

---

[1] Full text in German: www.konrad-adenauer.de/quellen/reden/1961-08-18-rede-essen.

deployed in the administrations of the new States. Two of the new States elected West German Minister Presidents.

The new States were subsumed under the term *"Beitrittsgebiet,"* accession territory, so the whole process was certainly not the unification of two equal partners; rather, it was clearly communicated that the new States were thought to knock on the door for admission, and then asked to be integrated into the already existing West German structures. Understandably, this caused a lot of bad blood and certainly still does.

After a meeting with U.S. Vice President Lyndon B. Johnson, Adenauer said, "What the Ulbricht regime did with the approval of the Warsaw Pact powers on August 13 was a breach of agreements and treaties, a violation of the Four Powers Status, a brutal act against our brothers and sisters in the Zone and in the eastern sector, an attack on freedom par excellence. But it was also . . . a first-rate declaration of bankruptcy for those in power in the Zone."[2] Here, we can already see how the wall served its purpose; it could be used to appeal to emotions, easily providing the image of a population behind a prison wall, where people were suppressed and forced into a socialist frame of mind.

When I was in Grade School, actually long before the wall had been built, we had to sing "Die Gedanken sind frei" by Pete Seeger (1966) virtually every morning. Talking about freely flowing thoughts which no scholar can map, no hunter can trap and no man can decry, and about foundations and structures that crumble and tumble, instilled quite a bit of fear in 8-year-old children![3]

It became also extremely important for the West German government to bring as many world leaders to the wall, so as to make sustainable the picture of inhuman suppression and exclusion. It was also important to show the victims of the wall—people risked their lives to escape, many succeeded, many failed. Many managed to

---

[2] TV address on 19 August. Full speech in German: www.konrad-adenauer.de/quellen/erklaerungen/1961-08-19-erklaerung-berlin.

[3] See www.youtube.com/watch?v=dbwQXVcbkU0 for a performance of this song. Leonard Cohen also used this song for a tour through Germany in 1976, thus pandering to the prevailing mood in Germany at the time.

get across with trucks simply breaking through the reinforcements, some escaped through tunnels, some built primitive airplanes, some tried to cross the Baltic Sea on boats and rafts. Many died in these attempts. The undisputed climax was President Kennedy's visit to Berlin when he said in his speech "Ich bin ein Berliner."

Fig.15.3: Pin from German-American Institute Museum/Michael Di Giovine

***

Walter Ulbricht went on to create a socialist culture, a socialist architecture, a socialist consciousness, in particular a socialist youth culture: Mr. Ulbricht's reaction to the emergence of the Beatles in the early Sixties was: "Is it really the case that we just have to imitate every piece of dirt that comes from the West? I think, comrades, with the monotony of the *je-je-je* [sic—he meant "yeah, yeah, yeah"], and what this all means, yes, you should put an end to it."

In the end, the measure to erect a wall was self-defeating: It created an intense longing for unification on both sides, a pressure within the GDR for freedom of movement.

The fall of the wall came after a prolonged economic crisis and pressure from the population which wanted to be able to travel. Two events precipitated the fall of the wall: On September 11, 1989, Hungary opened the border to Austria; many East Germans who happened to be there as tourists could leave Hungary into freedom. Within 3 weeks, 57,000 people managed to stream into Hungary and from there on to Austria and Germany. This created the widespread fear that the GDR would close the borders to its eastern neighboring states. People fled to Prague and climbed the fence to the German Embassy. Around 4,000 people waited for weeks to be able to travel to the West until Hans-Dietrich Genscher, the then-Foreign Minister, brought them the message that they could leave the embassy in trains via the GDR. Three times the embassy park was filled with nearly 5,000 people who were allowed to leave the country.

The fall then came surprisingly quick: On 9 November, Günter Schabowski, the GDR press secretary, stated in a press conference that a new regulation for GDR citizens for traveling to the West had been issued. He was caught off-guard when a reporter asked him about the time frame. He said as far as he knew this would be effective immediately. This led to a rush of thousands of GDR citizens to the border crossings, which made it impossible for the East German border guards to contain the movement.

The wall had come down.

Today, Berlin thrives on memorabilia of the Wall (Wallabilia?), there is a strong *"Ost-algie"*—nostalgia for the East—guided tours along the line which shows the former line of the wall, hotels with GDR furniture, small museums displaying East German items of everyday life.

"Berlin"

Berlin had been one of the cultural centers of Europe in the early 20th century. This came to an end with the emergence of the Nazis, the persecution of Jewish artists, Jewish scientists, and the Jewish population in general. Berlin took on a different role after the war; it became the symbol of the Cold War, the symbol of German unity, the ideological reference point in the competition of the West against the East. West Germany kept Berlin alive through films, art, and in songs: Marlene Dietrich sang the song *"Ich hab' noch einen Koffer in Berlin"*—"I left a little suitcase in Berlin"—also sung by Hildegard Knef and Katja Ebstein, two very popular stars in the Germany of the 50s, 60s, and 70s.

The site that stood for Berlin was the Brandenburg Gate as a German *lieu de memoir*, a term popularized by the French historian Pierre Nora, something like a place of national memory.

Yet, there is a much more interesting building in Berlin which symbolizes Berlin's development over the last century, and that is the Berlin castle and its telling history. Heavily damaged in WWII, the castle was demolished by the GDR in 1950 and turned into the "Marx-Engels Square" for state parades. The monarchical and imperial past of the German Reich was eradicated by the socialist state and converted into a site for propaganda and East German identity-building. For 23 years it was the site of the central marches and parades of the GDR. Later, in 1976, it became the site of the "Palace of the Republic," the official seat of the GDR parliament. It is somewhat ironic that a self-declared socialist state names the building housing the people's legislative institution the *"Palace* of the Republic." Part of the Marx-Engels-Platz was reserved for the parades. Yet, the vibrations of the heavy military vehicles during the parades were a threat to the glass façade of the Palace of the Republic, so the parades soon had to be held somewhere else. After unification, the building was closed due to asbestos contamination. In 2003, the German Bundestag decided that the building should be demolished. In 2013, construction of a new building was undertaken, the so-called Humboldt Forum. This was not just any new building in a contemporary style, but, strangely enough, a reconstruction of the Berlin castle in its old splendor, to be used as a representative building of the new, unified Germany. That is, as if the GDR had never existed. Just as the GDR wanted to eradicate the symbol of the German monarchy, so did the newly formed German republic eradicate the central piece of the GDR government, the "Palast der Republik." One wants to establish a tradition of German science and culture and connect the buildings of the museums, the castle, the Berlin Dome, and other central, traditional *lieux de memoir*. Interestingly enough, the first director of the Humboldt Forum was Neil MacGregor, the former Director of the British Museum, which points to the fact that the Humboldt Forum has similar objectives as the British Museum—that is, as a place of national memory and identity.

These examples show how buildings take on their own symbolic meaning and become an expression of power and authority, and how they undergo symbolic changes.

Monuments relating to events—or, in our case, buildings that replace other buildings—are not so much part of the events, but rather part of the narration and interpretation of events, the spinning of history. The objective side of "history"—the actual events of history—cannot be accessed or experienced any more. As soon as they are over, they must necessarily become part of the narrative. The subjective side—the narration and interpretation of the actual events—is what makes the monuments/memorials into true monuments/memorials. It is the appropriation of historical events for ideological intentions that transfers the event into narrative, into monument. The events are experienced by a collective, they remain in the collective consciousness, and are told and retold, formed and re-formed, devised and revised. If memory is enacted on the foundation of an ideology, or the memorial is used to convey a statement of supremacy, one may maintain that memory and narrative are never free of ideology, then monuments may be said to be petrified ideology.

So, the reconstructed Berlin castle will again be a focal point of German identity, of history, a celebration of German science and culture. The wall will become a distant memory, only kept alive by the pieces of the wall distributed all over the world and standing lonely in front of public buildings and will turn "history" into the "narrative of history."

Fig. 15.4: The reconstructed Berlin castle with the city's iconic TV tower in the background.

Memorialization and identity building are difficult concepts for post-World War II Germany. Germany started from zero with respect to identity-building as all "items of identity;" or, rather, if you will, the parameters of identity had been tainted and abused by the Nazis. The USA on the other hand has been able to create symbols and memorials of an unbroken history and thus create identity: the flag, the White House, the Lincoln memorial, and so on. Nevertheless, the heated debates about the Confederate flag or memorials of the Civil War show that here, too, there are cracks in the surface of cultural identity. And these debates too reveal structures of authority and power. It is the question of who rules over the past or over our national memory, which indeed creates identity. The first sentence of the British novel *The Go-Between* by L.P. Hartley (1953) reads "The past is another country." This holds true for the novel, and indeed, one's past is about as inaccessible as the GDR in its heyday, but the past with all its *lieux de mémoir* forms a country. Thus, Germany carries with it its past, the Holocaust,

Fig. 15.5: The author delivering this public lecture at West Chester University on September 19, 2019.

Museum/Michael Di Giovine

the wall—even if it has disappeared—, the 40 years of separation (which have led to what is being called "die Teilung in den Köpfen," the "separation in the heads") and so on. Berlin is being rebuilt; it is a still on-going process, but Berlin moves more and more toward a theme park, thriving on the past, yet not establishing a new identity: There is the Allied Museum, the Anti-War Museum, the Berlin Story Bunker, the GDR Motorbike Museum, the GDR Museum, Documentation Center Berlin Wall, at least seven memorials (Gedenkstätten), the Spy Museum, and so on. The Holocaust memorial and museum are meant to be attempts by Germany to come to terms with its past—but they are already tourist attractions. So, whatever the intentions are, the narrative will take over.

So, if the past is another country, we must accept as Hegel did, that historical facts and narrative are inseparable, that the narrative itself becomes history.

CHAPTER 16

Commemorating the Berlin Wall

Natalie Fenner

The commemoration of the Berlin Wall plays an active role in the lives of current citizens of Berlin. Such commemorations have taken a range of forms, from monuments to art, to narratives, and even to botany. The collective memory of Berliners who lived during the crisis and during the time of the fall is important; commemoration involves establishing a relationship between the things that people recognize and the event that took place, for example, the relationship between propaganda and art regarding the Berlin Wall and the art produced in reaction to it (e.g., stamps, postcards, pieces of wall) (see Manghani, 2008). There are also instances where there are obvious connections made between physical monuments and the Berlin Wall, and there are times where there are more intangible examples of memorialization.

Commemoration through Art

There are different art installations that commemorate the Berlin Wall, including the popular East Side Gallery and the contested installation called *"Dau Freiheit."*

The East Side Gallery is an open-air installation in Friedrichshain, Berlin. International artists painted over 100 large-format murals on the once-blank eastern side of the wall between 1990 and 2009,

Contributed by Natalie Fenner. © Kendall Hunt Publishing Company which together share common themes of peace, joy, and freedom of persecution (see also Anissa Kunchick's contribution to this volume, Chapter 25). Rather than serving as a blockade as it once did, this section of the wall now serves as a monument commemorating the liberation and resilience of the people of Berlin. As one of the largest open-air museums in the world, boasting iconic images such as Theirry Noir's colorful cartoon heads, the East Side Gallery sees over 3 million domestic and international visitors every year (East Side Gallery, n.d.).

"Dau Freiheit" (*Freiheit* means "freedom"), meanwhile, was conceived by Russian artist-filmmaker Ilya Khrzhanovsky to give visitors an experiential look at Berlin under Soviet-inspired rule. The centerpiece would be a towering recreation of the Berlin Wall constructed out of 900 12-feet tall concrete slabs. Intended to be unsettling, the temporary exhibit was to "emulate life in an unfamiliar country" (Solly, 2018): visitors would purchase a "visa" to gain entry to the city, pass through checkpoints; and swap their phones and electronics for internet-less devices that would act as tour guides. Visitors are taken through and shown films, concerts, and other interactive components. The exhibit as a whole was meant to evoke a reflexive sense of unease that East Berliners (and other citizens of Soviet-dominated societies) would have felt: "If the experience proves overwhelming, visitors can stop by viewing platforms situated throughout the pseudo-city. In addition to providing portals to the outside world, these windows mimic the Cold War platforms that allowed West Berliners to peek at their eastern counterparts" (Solly, 2018). The central event was that the wall would be pulled down on the 13th anniversary of the fall. However, just months before it was scheduled to open, the German government scrapped the plan amid outcry from politicians and locals that the installation hit too close from home; an OpEd in German newspaper *Tagesspiegel* argued, "People in a city who have suffered two dictatorships in a few decades need no instruction on what a dictatorship means" (qtd. Brown, 2018). Despite the city's attempts to address these issues, Khrzhanovsky ultimately relocated the installation to Paris in 2019 (Brown, 2019).

Beyond Berlin, the wall and its iconic fall has been memorialized in many different pieces of movable artwork, such as postcards and postage stamps. Our exhibit includes a collection of postcards purchased during and after the Berlin Wall period. Postcards are quintessential symbols of travel, and are often used as tangible souvenirs and mementos that "bring back" a destination to a person's home. They also create, solidify, and spread "tourist imaginaries" (Salazar & Graburn, 2014)—particular iconic images and expectations about a tourist destination—through their circulation. This collection of postcards serves as a deconstructed timeline of the Berlin Wall Crisis, while at the same time helping us to remember the events that occurred. Of particular interest is the postcard with (supposedly) authentic pieces of the Berlin Wall, purchased in 1998; not only could this type of postcard circulate imaginaries of the wall, but it could be used to circulate an actual piece of the wall itself.

With postcards come the postage stamps used to send them. Stamps themselves are often political commentaries, representations of important landscapes, people, and events of the nation that produced them. The exhibit contains First Day of Issue covers of a stamp commemorating the 1989 fall of the Berlin Wall—part

Fig. 16.1: Various forms of commemoration (left to right): postcards *(on loan from David Bolton)*; stamps; t-shirts; cherry blossoms.

of a larger "Celebrate the Century" series. Issued at the turn of the millennium by the U.S. Postal Service, the "Celebrate the Century" series of stamps provides iconic images of globally impactful events, mainly from the 20th century America—such as the Jitterbug, Apollo moon landing, Korean and Vietnam wars, Monopoly board game, and the Challenger explosion. Half of the stamps were chosen by the Citizens Stamp Advisory Committee and half by popular vote. One of comparatively few stamps not depicting a U.S. site, event or personality, the inclusion of the fall of the Berlin Wall in the series nevertheless reveals the importance it had on American culture and the role the United States played on its collapse.

Commemoration through Monuments

Art is not the only method of commemoration in Berlin. Vestiges of the Berlin Wall and other important buildings memorialize this period. A prime example is the Berlin Wall Memorial, a preserved section of the wall as it looked in the 1980s on Bernauer Strasse. The strip is just under one mile in length, but the power of it remains. The section of the wall reminds the citizens of Berlin of the trauma and pain their city went through, showing the side of dark tourism in Berlin.

Also located on Bernaurer Strasse, the Chapel of Reconciliation is another example of a monument dedicated to the Berlin Wall crisis. The modern Protestant chapel was built on the site of the former Church of the Reconciliation, a neo-Gothic construction completed in the late 1800s and damaged in World War II. Although rebuilt after the war, it was destroyed by the East German government in 1985 to expand the Berlin Wall, which had run directly in front of it. Indeed, although the church lay in the Soviet quadrant of Berlin, its parishioners were largely in the French quadrant on the West side, and consequently the church was not used for worship. Today, not only does the modern chapel stand as a monument to the brutality and destructiveness of the wall, but "before and after" images of the church are even featured on postcards, including one in our collection (see Fig. 16.2). Today, the chapel also serves as a place of worship, and regularly holds a prayer service for the lives lost to the wall.

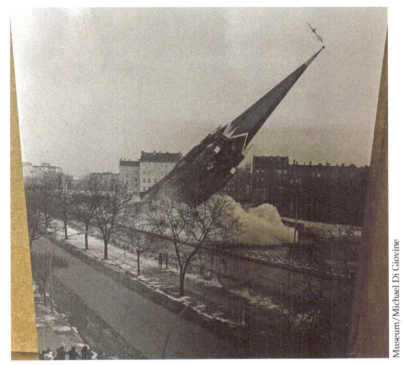

Fig. 16.2: Postcard showing the Soviet-led destruction of the Church of Reconciliation. *On loan from Brenda Gaydosh.*

Seasonal and Nature-Based Monuments

Not all monuments are of human construction. Lining Maurer Weg, a segment of the border where the Berlin Wall once stood are numerous cherry trees donated by Japan after the wall fell. Japanese TV Asahi collected over 140 million yen (around 1 million Euro) to gift the trees to several German cities, including Bonn, Berlin, Brandenburg, and Hamburg, to celebrate reunification and resilience. Beautiful yet ephemeral, the trees burst into a canopy of pink *sakura* (cherry blossoms) for around 2 weeks per year in April. There are cherry blossom festivals, or *Kirschblütenfest*, that also occur in Berlin where the flowers are supported by joy and the good spirit of Berlin. To symbolize these cherry trees, our exhibit features a line of cherry blossoms in vases (Fig. 16.3).

Fig. 16.3: Chapel of Reconciliation.

Fig. 16.4: Mauer Weg in springtime.

Commemorative Events

The exhibit also includes a white balloon, to evoke one of many episodes that memorialized the fall of the wall and celebrated the resilience of Berliners. To mark the 25th anniversary of the fall in

Fig. 16.5: Cherry blossoms and balloons represented in the exhibit

2014, an art installation, *Lichtgrenze 2014* ("Border of Light") was erected. It featured some 8,000 illuminated, white helium balloons that lined the path where the Berlin Wall once stood (Taylor, 2014). Perched on 12-foot poles to match the height of the wall and stretching for 15 km (9 miles)—the helium-filled balloons were released one by one after a concert at the Brandenburg Gate, to symbolize the breaching of the wall by crowds of protesters, as well as the individual efforts of Berliners on the ground to effect great change (Anon., 2014; Preuss, 2014). Other events at the 25th anniversary celebrations included a parade featuring the first Trabant car to cross the border, the word "peace" (*Frieden*) projected onto the Brandenburg Gate, concert, and speeches by prominent leaders including Chancellor Angela Merkel; Mikhail Gorbachev was also in attendance.

Fig. 16.6: *Lichtgrenze 2014.*

Conclusion: Memorializing or Creating "*Ostalgie*"?

As an iconic event, the fall of the Berlin Wall is commemorated in many ways and for different reasons. Remnants of the wall are preserved to serve as reminders of a difficult past—lest it be repeated yet again—or to reveal the resilience of the German people and celebrate reunification, though sometimes not without contestation. As a symbol of the victory of the United States and its allies over the Soviet bloc, it is commemorated on international stamps and postcards. There is serious interest in memorializing the lives lost and hardships endured, as shown by miles of cherry trees planted along the footprint of the wall and the construction of monuments. But this exists alongside a wistful sense of *"Ostalgie"*—nostalgia for the *Ost*, or East—particularly by the older generation discontent with the changes of modern day. Coined by East German standup comic Uwe Steimie in 1992 (DPA, 2012), "ostalgie" is a complex term that both references a sort of nostalgia—or longing for a romanticized past that never truly existed—but also a way of drawing distinctions valorizing East German ways of life in a time when much of the physical (but also social) remains of the GDR have been destroyed. Celebrating reunification and the fall of Cold War divisions, these various commemorations ultimately seem to present a time and political organization that has passed, while sometimes not recognizing the social realities of the present.

Bibliography

Anon. (2014). "Berlin Wall: Thousands of balloons released to mark fall." *BBC News*. Accessed on February 4, 2021 from https://www.bbc.com/news/world-europe-29974950.

Brown, K. (2018). "'We don't want to see a wall anymore': 'Berlin shuts down an artist's bold plan to rebuild the barrier.'" *Artnet News*. September 21. Accessed on February 4, 2021 from https://news.artnet.com/art-world/berlin-wall-dau-canceled-1353181

Brown, K. (2019). "A Russian filmmaker's plan to recreate the Berlin Wall was scuttled in Germany. Now, it will make its debut in Paris." *Artnet News*. January 4. Accessed on February 4, 2021 from https://news.artnet.com/art-world/dau-berlin-wall-project-paris-1431763.

DPA. (2012). Ostalgiker Uwe Steimle Bezeichnet Sich Als Kleinbürger. *Hannoversche Allemaine Zeitung*. October 12. Accessed on February 4, 2021 from https://www.haz.de/Nachrichten/Kultur/Uebersicht/Ostalgiker-Uwe-Steimle-bezeichnet-sich-als-Kleinbuerger.

East Side Gallery. (n.d.). Website. Accessed on February 3, 2021 from http://www.eastsidegallery-berlin.com/

Manghani, S. (2008). *Image critique and the fall of the Berlin Wall*. Chicago: Intellect Books.

Preuss, A. (2014). "Somber, hopeful ceremonies mark 25 years since the Berlin Wall fell." *CNN*. November 9. Accessed on February 23, 2021 from https://www.cnn.com/2014/11/09/world/europe/fall-of-berlin-wall-25-years-on/index.html

Salazar, N., & Graburn, N. (2014). *Tourist imaginaries: Anthropological approaches*. Oxford: Berghahn.

Solly, M. (2018). "An immersive art installation will temporarily resurrect the Berlin Wall." *Smithsonian Magazine*. Accessed on

February 4, 2021 from https://www.smithsonianmag.com/smart-news/immersive-art-installation-will-temporarily-resurrect-berlin-wall-180970168/

Taylor, A. (2014). "Lichtgrenze 2014: Commemorating the fall of the Berlin Wall." *The Atlantic.* November 9. Accessed on February 23, 2021 from https://www.theatlantic.com/photo/2014/11/lichtgrenze-2014-commemorating-the-fall-of-the-berlin-wall/100849/

CHAPTER 17

The Commercialization of the Berlin Wall

Foster W. Krupp and Christian Sabree

The Berlin Wall continues to be culturally relevant in its afterlife, though it has changed both physically and symbolically. In the 30 years since its fall, the wall's remnants and the spaces it used to occupy have been transformed into both new material culture as well as sites of commercialization, tourism, and memorialization. On the one hand, the remaining physical pieces of the wall that are still standing, as well as the areas in which it previously stood, have become a heritage and tourism site, a draw to those who seek to experience the wall (if not its horrors) themselves. On the other hand, its images and even its fragments themselves have entered the marketplace as commodities, bought and sold by those who want to own a piece of history. The Berlin Wall's fall may have been a moment of joy and happiness but, in turn, it has also given way to exploitation.

Tourism is a significant way that the era of the Berlin Wall, as well as the moment of its fall, have been capitalized on for monetary profit. Such tourist products include the Berlin Wall Bike Tour, which according to the tour operator's website, takes visitors to highlights such as the "Berlin Wall Memorial, Former Death Strip, No-man's-land watchtower, Site of tunnels and escapes, Stasi Records Agency, and more" (Fat Tire Tours, n.d.). TripAdvisor advertises other options for viewing the Berlin Wall: "Berlin Highlights

Contributed by Foster W. Krupp and Christian Sabree.
© Kendall Hunt Publishing Company

and Hidden Sites Historical Walking Tour, Red Buses Berlin Hop-On Hop-Off Bus with Boat Option, and Third Reich and Berlin Wall History 3-Hour Bike Tour" (Trip Advisor, n.d.). This last one couples not one, but two, dark periods in Berlin's history, seemingly turning them both into a brief and rather enjoyable half-day leisure ride through the cityscape of Berlin.

Tourism to the Berlin Wall is an example of a modern dark tourism site. Dark tourism is described as "visitations to places where tragedies or historically noteworthy death has occurred and that continue to impact our lives" (Sharpley & Stone, 2009; Tarlow, 2005, p. 48). Even though the Berlin Wall was a site of conflict and death during the Cold War, curious tourists still have a strong desire to visit such sites and memorials in Berlin. Some may do so out of veneration and respect for the suffering of the people, and some may do it to gain better understanding of the difficulties and complex history of the era, but others do it out of a somewhat morbid curiosity. Dark tourism sites like the Berlin Wall raise many questions, especially on the ethics of capitalizing a negative aspect of Germany and Berlin's history to international tourists. There are thoughts from stakeholders who lived with the Berlin Wall that tourism and souvenirs minimize the hardships of the Berlin Wall they experienced at the time. Yet despite the dark undertones, this may still have the positive benefit of enlightening the people who desire to tour Berlin and understand, and come in contact with, a piece of history themselves.

With tourism comes souvenirs—trinkets and other commodities that international visitors purchase to bring their experiences of the wall back home. Images of the wall are found on shirts, mugs, posters, and other types of merchandise—many of which are featured in this exhibit. These, as well as the embodied experiences at the site itself, produce what Salazar and Graburn call "tourism imaginaries"—socially transmitted representations of a place that interact with peoples' own imaginings, which are then used as "meaning-making and world-shaping devices" (2014, p. 1). In short, they create our understandings of what the place is, what it should be, and what its significance is for the tourist. What is important about souvenirs of the wall on such mundane objects is that it conflates, or associates together, the dark history of the wall with stereotyped symbols of broader German culture, such as the beer stein on display; it makes us associate these two very different aspects of Germany's history and culture as what makes "German-ness."

Interestingly, the beer stein was produced before German reunification; it is stamped "Made in West Germany" on it. However, the magnet on display, which depicts Checkpoint Charlie and is much newer, was actually made in China and purchased on the Internet. Placed together, these two artifacts reveal the interesting ways in which the wall, and its imaginaries, have globalized; not only do they circulate across the world—bought and carried back to one's home country like the West German beer stein souvenir, or purchased in West Chester through an international website such as eBay from a seller abroad—but it also shows how the production of these objects have also globalized. China is a leading importer of low-cost, mass-produced items, particularly such souvenirs that serve to remind those non-Berliners who purchased them of a land many workers in the Chinese company who produced it have never seen. Yet the purchase not only helps support the Chinese economy, but also the German economy as well. While this may not seem extraordinary, it does point to the changes these 30 years

Fig. 17.1: Commercialization of the Berlin Wall exhibit

Fig. 17.2: Pieces of the wall sold to tourists. *On loan from Jordan Schugar.*

have brought: the Berlin Wall—which during its existence cut off East Germany and its citizens from the global market and much of the world—has now, though tourism, entered the global market, and helps mobilize people from around the world to visit the place and contribute to several places' economic development.

Indeed, the Berlin Wall has become a cultural heritage site, and with it, a commodified draw to international tourists. But in the 30 years since the Fall of the Berlin Wall, the use of what remains of the wall has drastically changed. With the Berlin Wall dividing about 155 kilometers, it is little surprise that there are many of remnants of it to this day. One estimate claims that there is enough of the Berlin Wall to ". . . give one golf-ball-sized piece of the Berlin Wall to every fifteen people on the planet" (Veronese, 2019). With so many physical remains, it makes sense that the Berlin Wall would be commercialized. Having transformed from a border wall, these fragments of the Berlin Wall now exist as "pieces of history" with both a monetary and symbolic value in the cultural landscape.

Fig. 17.3: Chipping pieces off the wall in 1990. *On loan from Peter Loedel.*

Even in the immediate aftermath of the Berlin Wall's fall, the seeds of commercialization emerged. People in Germany began this process, with these "wall-peckers focused particularly on sections of the border wall on Niederkirchnerstraße, breaking it into small pieces for sale to tourists in the months following reunification" (Harrison, 2013, p. 178). Wall fragments could be bought in the streets, or hammers could be rented to break off a piece of the wall independently. Several of these fragments, collected by hand by people associated with West Chester University, are on display at the beginning of this exhibition (see Fig.s 17.3 and 17.4). This type of souvenir is still popular to this day, and fragments of the Berlin Wall with certificates of authenticity can also be easily purchased on websites like Amazon.com and eBay.com from different sellers. These pieces can be purchased in a variety of forms, ranging from refrigerator magnets to relic-like acrylic cases.

These fragments have a symbolic value that is created by the public memory of the Berlin Wall, which adds to their value. After all,

CHAPTER 17 The Commercialization of the Berlin Wall

Fig. 17.4: Pieces of the Berlin Wall collected by WCU professors.

in the basest sense, they are simply pieces of concrete with spray paint. But the physical connection these pieces have with the history of the Berlin Wall and the greater Cold World culture in the Western world makes them worthy of ownership and control (Baudrilliard, 1994). With a piece of the wall, a collector or tourist gets to become part of the history of the wall; even if it is only in the Berlin Wall's afterlife. These fragments are frequently "... treated as holy relics that bespoke our deliverance from the Cold War" (Ladd, 2001, p. 8). This can also be seen in how many fragments are sold like medieval relics, with a stamped number and a protective case that still allows physical touch, such as one in this exhibit.

The Berlin Wall is also commercialized in other ways. The popularity of homeopathic remedies has lead at least one company to make a medicinal pill allegedly using diluted, ground-up pieces of the wall. The supposed effects of this remedy include, but are not limited to, relief from headaches, asthma, and insomnia (Fig. 17.5).

Toy companies, like the LEGO Group, use the Berlin Wall to sell toys. Some collectable toy cars even come packaged with pieces of the Berlin Wall, while the LEGO Architecture Berlin set includes special printed pieces of Berlin Wall fragments. Perhaps aimed at educating children, or perhaps as a fun way to engage in some

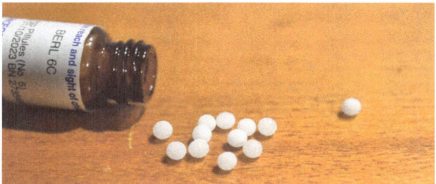

Fig. 17.5: Homeopathic remedy, apparently made from pulverized pieces of the wall.

"armchair tourism," the LEGO Architecture Berlin set comes with a thick multilingual book that explains each of the disparate sites featured, much like a tourist guidebook does to those actually exploring the site. And like the tourist itineraries mentioned above, it moves between past and present, dark periods of history and prouder, modern periods, as the little LEGO pieces of the Berlin Wall are juxtaposed with models of the Reichstag building and the GDR-constructed TV tower—which itself was used by the socialist government as a tourist destination to reveal its supposed modernity and power. With so many pieces of the wall circulating (authentic or fakes), and with some many different media through which imaginaries of the wall and its time period meld with other images and symbols of Germany, there are seemingly endless possibilities for Berlin Wall commercialization, and with its continued cultural relevance and bulk of fragments, there seems to be a sustained desire to use it in different ways for profit.

Commercialization is a clear and significant aspect of the afterlife of the Berlin Wall. Because there is value in these Berlin Wall pieces, there will also be a market for them. The Berlin Wall is a somewhat unusual cultural heritage site, because in the 30 years since its destruction, it continues to be sold and used to sell products worldwide. Perhaps Western capitalism did win even on the eastern side of Germany, because there is arguably nothing more capitalistic than using the power of culture and history to sell pieces of spray-painted concrete.

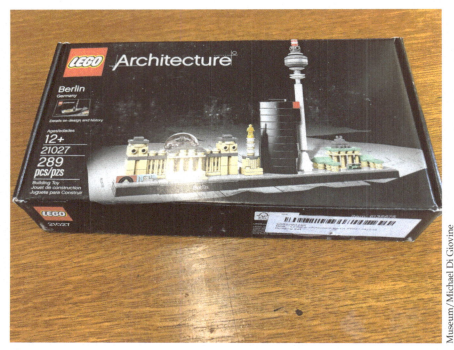

Fig. 17.6: LEGO Berlin set. *On loan from Alexander Di Giovine.*

Bibliography

Baudrilliard, J. (1994). "The system of collecting" In John Elsner & Roger Cardinal (eds.). *Cultures of collecting*. Reaktion Books.

Fat Tire Tours (n.d.). "Explore the Best of Berlin with Fat Tire Tours." *Explore Berlin | Bike and Segway Tours | Rentals | Fat Tire Tours*, www.fattiretours.com/berlin.

Harrison, R. (2013). *Heritage: Critical approaches*. New York: Routledge.

Ladd, B. (2001). *Berlin: A modern history*. London: Penguin.

Manghani, S. (2008). *Image critique and the fall of the Berlin Wall*. Bristol: Intellect Books.

Salazar, N. & Graburn, N. (2014). *Tourism imaginaries: Anthropological approaches*. Oxford: Berghahn.

Sharpley, R. & Stone, P. H. (2009). *The darker side of travel: The theory and practice of dark tourism.* Clevedon: Channel View Publications.

Tarlow, P. (2005). Dark tourism: The appealing 'dark' side of tourism and more. In M. Novelli (ed.). *Niche tourism: Contemporary issues, trends and cases* (pp. 47–57). Oxford: Elsevier.

TripAdvisor (n.d.). "Berlin: Tours and Tickets". Retrieved May 9, 2019 from https://www.tripadvisor.com/Attraction_Products-g187323-Berlin.html

Veronese, K. (2019). "Your piece of the Berlin Wall is not special." Io9. December 16, 2015. Accessed April 10, 2019. https://io9.gizmodo.com/your-piece-of-the-berlin-wall-is-not-special-5934159.

CHAPTER 18

The Berlin Wall in Popular Culture

Brianna A. Eldridge

The fall of the Berlin Wall 30 years ago was a momentous occasion, as it signaled the beginning of the end of the Cold War. At the time, the event was a symbol of triumph over an oppressive regime, but as time goes on, the way we remember the wall changes and it begins to take on different meanings. In many ways, the Berlin Wall today is less about the struggle that East Germans were forced to suffer for 28 years, although certain narratives still present this. Tracing the iconic Berlin Wall's presence in popular culture, this exhibit showcases a variety of media—from music to stage productions to film to a diversity of novels.

One of the first pop culture references that people often think of when recalling the Berlin Wall is the 1979 Pink Floyd album, *The Wall*, but the band did not originally write the album about the wall. In an interview with radio DJ Tommy Vance (1979), lead singer Roger Waters explains how he "became very conscious of a wall between us and our audience and so this record started out as being an expression of those feelings." He explains how the shows became an isolating experience not only between the band and the audience, but also between himself and the band. But although Pink Floyd did not originally intend for the album to be about the Berlin Wall, many fans have interpreted it that way. Pink Floyd eventually began to recognize not only the cultural significance of

Fig. 18.1: The Berlin Wall in Popular Culture exhibit

the album, but also the political and historical significance that the album began to symbolize. While The Wall may not fit the Berlin Wall exactly, there are still many similarities that can be seen between the GDR and the song's main character, Pink. The GDR is forced to reconcile with its Nazi past and adapt to the practices of the Soviet Union who, much like Pink's mother, gives them very little freedom. Pink's failures in life can be compared to the rising tensions that marked the Cold War through the 1950s; both became increasingly suspicious of those around them and eventually they built the wall "simultaneously blocking out and hiding from the rest of the world" (Gorman, 2015).

A couple years before the fall of the Berlin Wall, Roger Waters was asked if he would ever create another show for *The Wall* and "Waters said no, but quipped that he 'might do it outdoors if they ever take the wall down in Berlin'" (Blake, 2008, p. 343). Eight months after the fall of the Berlin Wall, Pink Floyd and countless other artists held a concert in Berlin and, 2 months after the performance, a live album and a VHS tape were released. This is one of the many examples of how the meaning of objects or events changes over time. The Berlin Wall used to be a symbol of division, but has now become a symbol of people unifying under extreme circumstances.

There have been multiple movies about the Berlin Wall and one of the most notable is the 2003 film, *Goodbye Lenin!* (Becker, 2003). The film is set in 1990 and is about a family who attempts to convince their mother that the Berlin Wall has not fallen and that they are still living in communist East Berlin to prevent his mother from having another life-threatening heart attack. *Goodbye, Lenin!* gives an interesting insight into what East Berlin was like once the West began taking over after the fall. It also shows how the communists viewed the wall as beneficial and necessary for self-preservation; they saw it as something that kept American influences out rather than forcing people to stay in East Berlin.

Die Stille nach dem Schuß, or *The Silence after the Shot* (Schlöndorff, 2000), was released in Germany in 2000 and in the United States under the title *The Legend of Rita* in 2001. Based on the lives of various members of the Red Army Faction terrorist organization

(RAF) operating in West Germany, the movie presents a different side of the Wall by featuring a woman named Rita who is a RAF terrorist. Rita escapes to East Berlin, which is the opposite of where many people tried to escape to, so she could create a new life. Presenting the opposite view is that of the character Lorraine Broughton in *Atomic Blonde*. This film was released in 2017 and is about an MI-6 spy who is sent on a dangerous mission to retrieve information from behind the Berlin Wall and break up an espionage ring that is suspected of killing a fellow agent. While *The Legend of Rita* tries to be historically accurate and give audiences a different perspective, *Atomic Blonde* portrays the Berlin Wall as just a historical backdrop.

Hedwig and the Angry Inch (Mitchell, 1998) is a rock musical about a transgender East German that originally debuted off-Broadway 1998 and was adapted into a film in 2001. It was officially produced on Broadway in 2014 with Neil Patrick Harris starring as the main character, Hedwig, who was born as Hansel Schmidt in East Berlin. Before her botched gender reassignment surgery, she met an American soldier named Luther Robinson who married her so she could leave East Berlin. Unfortunately, not only does her husband leave her on their first wedding anniversary, but the Berlin Wall also comes down on the same day and she feels as if her sacrifices were in vain.

Hedwig helps a young teen, Tommy, become the famous singer he had always dreamed of being, but when he finds out that she was not born female and her surgery left her with an "angry inch," he leaves her and takes credit for her songs. In retaliation, she creates her "internationally ignored" glam rock band and follows Tommy's cross-country tour. While the Berlin Wall is only a small detail in Hedwig's story, it is used as a symbol for Hedwig herself. In the song, "Tear Me Down," Hedwig's husband Yitzhak compares the Berlin Wall, as the most reviled symbol of a divided city, to Hedwig; both are hated, graffitied, and spit upon. Yitzhak likens the divide between East and West to slavery and freedom, and, importantly, between man and woman. They use the liminality of the Berlin Wall to symbolize how Hedwig is neither man nor woman, and how she is unsure of who she is. The wall is used as a metaphoric character trait rather than as an actual event that affected people.

The way that some people have coped with living with the wall has been by writing books to explain to other people what it was like. *The Other Side of the Wall* is a nonfiction graphic novel written by Simon Schwartz (2015). Schwartz was born in 1982 in East Berlin and the story follows his family as they decide to escape to the other side of the wall. Throughout the graphic novel, his parents struggle with their families' reaction to their decision and trying to avoid the Stasi.

Other books are written to memorialize, such as *The Wall* by Tom Clohosy Cole (2015). This is an illustrated children's book that was published for the 25th anniversary of the fall of the Berlin Wall. The little boy, his mother, and his sister were stuck in East Berlin while his father was in the West and it shows how families were separated by the Berlin Wall. The author can explain the relevance and meaning in a way that young children will be able to comprehend. By having the family dig a hole under the wall, Tom Clohosy Cole shows how people could escape East Germany in bizarre and interesting ways. In this book, the little boy digs a hole to West Berlin and when a Stasi officer stops him and his family from escaping, the little boy shows the officer a picture of his father and then they are allowed to go free. *The Wall* gives readers a happy ending while also showing the pain of having a family torn apart.

An issue that many tragedies face is the romanticizing of the event. The young adult novel, *Going Over* (Kephart, 2015), is about two star-crossed lovers named Ada and Stefan who are separated by the Berlin Wall in 1983. The only way they can be together is if Stefan can make the daring escape from East to West Berlin. The author takes a terrible time in history and tries to create a tragic teenage love story when the Berlin Wall had a much bigger effect on those who lived in the east and west.

The fall of the Berlin Wall was brought about by a complicated series of social and political events that is explored in this exhibition, but in popular culture it is often simplified and even mischaracterized. One example is the attribution that 1980s actor-singer David Hasselhoff was at least partially responsible for the collapse of the wall (see, for example, Hunter, 2018; NPR Staff, 2014). David Hasselhoff was a German-American actor, producer, and singer who became famous for a string of popular television shows in the 1970s to 1990s, including the long-running soap opera *The Young and the Restless* (1975–1982); the adventure series *Knight Rider* (1982–1986); and iconic *Baywatch* (1989–2000), which represented the apex of his fame. During his time on *Baywatch*, Hasselhoff also reinvented himself as a singer in Europe, with several triple platinum albums; he was particularly popular in Germany. In 1988, he released his single *Looking for Freedom*, which became popular in the year leading to the fall of the Wall, as it became synonymous with East Germany's struggle. His eponymous single was at the top of the charts all through the summer in Germany, and Hasselhoff himself suggested it was partially this desire for freedom that created the momentum for the fall (see McArthur, 2018), though in a recent interview with *Time* magazine he laughed off the suggestion (Waxman 2019). Seemingly to confirm this, a month after the fall of the wall, Hasselhoff was invited to sing the song at the Brandenburg Gate to a crowd of around one million reunited Germans on New Year's Eve 1989; Dana Cressler (Chapter 14, this book) recalls that event. The song, sung as Hasselhoff stood in a bucket crane over the Wall, became a type of anthem for the reunification of Germany, and he remained popular in Germany through the turn of the millennium. The concert permanently created a connection between the fall and David Hasselhoff, leading his story to be inexorably intertwined with that of the wall. Indeed, decades after the fall, Hasselhoff became an advocate for historic preservation of the remaining portions of the wall against developers in Berlin (Hartley, 2013).

The Berlin Wall has taken on many different meanings since its fall in 1989 (Sonnevend, 2016). In some interpretations, it has become its own character and in others it is used as a backdrop (sometimes even for a historically inaccurate story); it has even been used as a metaphor for other issues. Each time it is referenced in pop culture, the meaning of the wall is changed and molded to fit the story of which it becomes a part. The wall, and its memory, is therefore always in a constant state of flux, and we must be conscious of its importance for those who lived through its existence.

Bibliography

Angle, B. "Roger Waters explains the imagery and symbolism behind the wall live, his update of the Pink Floyd classic." *Guitarworld*. November 06, 2013. Accessed May 10, 2019. https://www.guitarworld.com/magazine/roger-waters-explains-imagery-and-symbolism-behind-wall-live-his-update-pink-floyd-classic.

Becker, W. (2003). *Good-Bye, Lenin!* Film. Distributed by X-Filme Creative Pool.

Blake, M. (2008). *Comfortably numb: The inside story of Pink Floyd*. New York: Da Capo Press.

Cole, T. C. (2015). *The wall*. Surrey: Templar Publishing.

Gorman, D. (2015). "Another brick in the Berlin Wall: Pink Floyd's The Wall and East Germany's place in history." *Tangents USA blog*, February 6. Accessed on May 29, 2019 from https://tangentsusa.wordpress.com/2015/02/06/another-brick-in-the-berlin-wall-pink-floyds-and-germany/

Hartley, E. (2013). "David Hasselhoff's role in the Fall of the Berlin Wall." *The Guardian*, March 19. Accessed on January 29, 2021 from https://www.theguardian.com/commentisfree/2013/mar/19/david-hasselhoff-berlin-wall-fall

Hunter, R. (2018). "How David Hasselhoff brought down the Berlin Wall." *SBS*, November 9, 2018. https://www.sbs.com.au/guide/article/2018/11/07/how-david-hasselhoff-brought-down-berlin-wall.

Kephart, B. (2015). *Going over*. San Francisco, CA: Chronicle Books LLC.

McArthur, K. (2018). "Did David Hasselhoff bring down the Berlin Wall?" *Sandemans New Europe*. Accessed on January 29, 2021 from https://www.neweuropetours.eu/blog/history/did-david-hasselhoff-bring-down-the-berlin-wall/

Mitchell, J. C. (1998). *Hedwig and the angry inch*. Original Broadway Musical.

NPR Staff (2014). "How Mr. Hasselhoff tour down this Wall." *NPR*. November 9. Accessed on January 29, 2021 from www.npr.org/2014/11/09/362595983/how-mr-hasselhoff-tore-down-this-wall.

Schlöndorff, V. (2000). *Die Stille nach dem Schuß. (The Legend of Rita).* Film. Distributed by Kino International.

Schwartz, S. (2015). *The Other Side of the Wall.* Minneapolis: Graphic Universe.

Sonnevend, J. (2016). *Stories without borders: The Berlin Wall and the making of a global iconic event.* Cambridge: Oxford University Press.

Vance, T. (1979). "The Wall—Song By Song—1979". Edited by Jeremy Crampton. *The Pink Floyd Fan Club.* Accessed on May 10, 2019 at http://www.pink-floyd.org/artint/98.htm

Waxman, O. (2019). 'I Was Just a Man Who Sang a Song About Freedom': 30 years later, David Hasselhoff looks back on his surprising role in the Fall of the Berlin Wall." *Time.* November 7. Accessed on January 29, 2021 from https://time.com/5714602/david-hasselhoff-berlin-wall-fall/

CHAPTER 19

Concerts at the Berlin Wall

Jim McAllister

"General Secretary Gorbachev, if you seek peace, if you seek prosperity for the Soviet Union and Eastern Europe, if you seek liberalization, come here to this gate. Mr. Gorbachev, open this gate! Mr. Gorbachev, tear down this wall!" What does this quote have to do with concerts at the Berlin Wall? This excerpt is from a speech given by President Ronald Reagan on June 12, 1987 (see Robinson, 2007), which was four days after the completion of a 3-day concert entitled "The Concert for Berlin." That concert, which featured the Eurythmics, David Bowie, and Genesis created an uprising of East German youth, which was met with brute authoritative force by East German officials. Other musical artists also contributed to the rebellion of East German youth against their Communist leaders; those artists include David Hasselhoff, Bruce Springsteen, Leonard Bernstein, Roger Waters, and U2 (Chase, 2007; Fisher, 2016).

The Berlin Wall was not only a geographical division between East and West Germany; the Wall itself also served as a political, cultural, and symbolic divide. The 1987 "Concert for Berlin" showcased the political and cultural divide between East and West Germany. German entrepreneur Peter Schwenkow was the promoter and producer of the concert. The decision to hold the concert at the Reichstag was according to Schwenkow, "an act of revenge." Schwenkow had previously been interrogated by East German border guards when he attempted to ascertain information about an incident in 1977 where some of Tina Turner's crew members were killed travelling through East Germany. The concert was going to

Contributed by Jim McAllister. © Kendall Hunt Publishing Company be broadcast on the radio station RIAS2 throughout East and West Germany. All three of the artists had given their permission to have the concert broadcast in its entirety, which was not common practice in the 1980s because fans would be able to record the songs instead of buying the albums. But this concert was about more than music. The wall created a symbolic divide between communism and capitalism. These concerts, along with the Perestroika and Glasnost policies introduced by Mikhail Gorbachev, were working hand in hand to bring down this wall.

Perestroika and Glasnost were two policies that opened the Soviet Union to the Western world and loosened state control within the Soviet Union and its surrounding states. Concert performances in 1987 ("Concert for Berlin"), 1988 (Bruce Springsteen), and 1989 (David Hasselhoff) at the wall were important symbolic events that coincided with the eventual collapse of the wall (Chase, 2007). The impact these events had on the collapse is debatable, but they all undeniably radicalized East German youth and the world took notice. *The New York Times* on June 9, 1987 reported that around a thousand "club-wielding policemen charged a crowd" of nearly 4000 young East German rock fans, who, while listening to an open-air concert in West Berlin, chanted "The wall must go!" It was the third night in a row of violence (Anon, 1987).

Genesis had performed on the final night of the concert, but the biggest star of the concert was David Bowie, who performed on the second evening. Bowie had moved to West Berlin in 1976 and stayed through 1979. Bowie released three albums doing his time in Berlin, the most popular one being *Heroes* in 1977. The title track of that album shares the same name as the title. The song is written about two young lovers on each side of the wall and their quest to be together. Bowie performed *Heroes* that June night in 1987 after telling the crowd, "We send our wishes to all our friends who are on the other side of the Wall" (Fisher, 2016).

The other side of the Wall finally got its chance to see an official concert when Bruce Springsteen performed in Weissensee on July 16, 1988. The East German communist youth organization, the Freie Deutsche Jugend (FDJ) was working against the efforts to bring concerts into East Germany after the 1987 "Concert for Berlin." The FDJ decided to offer concerts they could control in the Weissensee district park. The first concerts were held in June 1988, with Joe Cocker and Bryan Adams playing to large crowds. Bruce Springsteen was approached by the FDJ to perform in July based on the belief that he had donated a printing press to a leftist group in Nicaragua, one aligned with East German officials. FDJ officials labeled the concert "Heart for Nicaragua." Springsteen's camp complained about the branding around the venue and the FDJ removed it with little objection. Crowd estimates for the concert range from 200,000 to 500,000 East Germans. The symbolism of over 200,000 East Germans waving American flags and rocking out to "The Boss" in a Soviet-controlled city carried more weight than any political speech. Springsteen did give a speech while performing *Chimes of Freedom*, however, in which he said, "I want to tell you I'm not here for or against government; I came to play rock 'n' roll for you East Berliners in the hope that one day all the barriers will be torn down" (Kirschbaum, 2008).

That brings us to 1989, when the Wall finally came down. David Hasselhoff released his hit single *Looking for Freedom* during the summer of 1989. German music fans loved the song and it stayed at the top of German music charts for eight weeks. In an interview with NPR host Rachel Martin, Hasselhoff explained,

> And then I found out later talking to an East Berlin guy and a West Berlin guy, one guy says, you know, he thinks I'm from East Berlin. He thinks that "Looking for Freedom" was just a song in West Berlin. I go, yeah it was. It was just a pop song. He says, no it wasn't. It was our hymn. It was our anthem. It was our song of hope (Hasselhoff & Martin, 2014).

Hasselhoff was invited to play a concert on New Year's Eve 1989, which was two months after the official collapse of the wall in November. The Hasselhoff concert was the second concert to be held at the Wall after the collapse. Leonard Bernstein, famed Jewish-American composer, played a Christmas concert at the Wall, where he led a performance of Beethoven's *Ninth Symphony* and changed the "Ode to Joy" to an "Ode to Freedom." Choir members assembled from East and West Germany as well as France, Great Britain, the Soviet Union, and the United States. Other concerts that took place after the collapse include Roger Waters performing Pink

Fig. 19.1: Listening to David Hasselhoff on New Year's Eve at the wall. *Photo by Dana Cressler.*

Floyd's *The Wall*, which Waters had almost entirely written himself. U2 also performed at the Brandenburg Gate in 2009 to celebrate the 10-year anniversary of the collapse.

The question remains unanswered about the impact pop culture had on the collapse of the Berlin Wall. Did the combination of extreme policies enacted by Gorbachev in response to a failing Soviet Union, and a sudden rise of rock 'n' roll in East Germany contribute to the collapse of the Wall? Authoritative measures were taken during the 1987 Berlin concert, yet there was minimal upheaval during Springsteen's concert in East Berlin one year later. The use of music to bridge a divide that had been in place since 1961 is more than just symbolism. The Berlin Wall would have come down eventually but the power of music, which brought together East and West Germans starting in 1987, did more than any political speech. So, yes President Reagan, Mr. Gorbachev had to "take down that wall."

Bibliography

Anon. (1987). "Police and rock fans battle in East Berlin." *New York Times*, Section A, p. 9, June 9. Accessed July 9, 2021. https://www.nytimes.com/1987/06/09/world/police-and-rock-fans-battle-in-east-berlin.html

Chase, J. (2007). "87 Concert was a genesis of East German Rebellion." *dw.com*. April 7. Accessed September 3, 2019. https://www.dw.com/en/87-concert-was-a-genesis-of-east-german-rebellion/a-2663850

Fisher, M. (2016). "David Bowie at the Berlin Wall: The incredible story of a concert and its role in history." *Vox.com*. January 11. Accessed September 3, 2019. https://www.vox.com/2016/1/11/10749546/david-bowie-berlin-wall-heroes

Hassellhoff, D., & Martin, R. (2014). *How Mr. Hasselhoff tore down this wall* (November 9).

Kirschbaum, E. (2008). "Memories of how Springsteen rocked Berlin." Reuters. Accessed August 23, 2021 from https://www.reuters.com/article/us-germany-springsteen/memories-of-how-springsteen-rocked-berlin-idUSL1334031920080716

Robinson, P. (2007). "Tear down this wall." *archives.gov*. Summer. Accessed September 29, 2019. https://www.archives.gov/publications/prologue/2007/summer/berlin.html

CHAPTER 20

The Persistence of Division

Brittany Siemon

Most believed that after the Berlin Wall was torn down and many steps to reintegrate the two parts of Berlin and Germany were executed, that the people were no longer divided. However, both statistics and physical images exist to say otherwise. Not only do statistics show a marked division, but even interviews and surveys there to still be a divide between the peoples.

Fig. 20.1: The Persistence of Division

Christa Mientus-Schirmer from Berlin's city government explains, "Berlin was divided into two parts for over 40 years. And although we've made a lot of progress in the 20 years since the wall fell, we haven't had the money we would have liked to equalize the two parts of the city" (Hartley, 2013). While these divisions may not be visible from the ground level, they are still prominent—particularly from above. In 2012, the International Space Station orbiting Earth's atmosphere captured an image of Berlin by Canadian commander Chris Hadfield (Fig. 20.2). Where the lights meet is where the Berlin Wall used to stand, showing how former East Berlin still suffers from unequal distribution of resources. The yellow lights show East Berlin and the green lights show West Berlin. The eastern part still uses sodium-vapor lamps that emit a yellower color, while the west uses fluorescent lamps that are white (and have taken on a green hue from space). Installed during the FRG, fluorescent lights are more energy-efficient, cost-effective, and sustainable, but weren't available to the East when the wall was up. Daniela Augenstein, from the city's street department, says: "The western Federal Republic of Germany long favoured non-sodium lamps on the grounds of cost, maintenance and carbon emissions" (Hartley, 2013).

Fig 20.2: "Berlin at Night," photographed by Canadian astronaut and International Space Station Commander Chris Hadfield.

Apart from the divisions in the physicality of the city, there are many divisions in the operation of everyday lives in Berlin and Germany as a whole. After the fall of the wall in 1989, birth rates significantly decreased as much of the East went bankrupt and the citizens could not afford to have any more children (Zeit, 2014). Along with low birth rates came a notable flight from the land, as the younger generation of East Berliners and East Germans migrated westward in search of better work opportunities, leaving behind an abundance of older people and a lack of children. As when the two sides were divided, western Germany still has higher employment rates, in part because of the migration of so many young Easterners.

Along with the move of many East Germans, it started to become clear that language itself had changed in the decades-long separation, with distinct dialects being formed. In some cases, there are seven different names for one single object (Zeit, 2014). Language is an important component of identity. This linguistic divide both marks and creates a strong identity separation between the easterners and the westerners, and is sometimes is celebrated as each region's distinct heritage. In a sense, the temporary separation into East and West Germany has enriched the language even more (Zeit, 2014).

While the wall was up, the Communist party in the East strongly supported child care and immunizations. Most parents, including mothers, had a job to support the family, which in turn had the government in the East establish child care facilities, which are still operational and well known for excellent child care even today (Noack, 2014). In the West however, mothers typically stayed home. The East also pushed and demanded the immunization of children, while the West still saw as optional and not quite as important. Even today children in the East receive better childcare and have a higher rate of immunization (Noack, 2014).

Germany and specifically Berlin may not physically divided anymore, but there are still many ways in which their everyday lives are still affected. A survey which was completed for the 25th anniversary of the Fall of the Berlin Wall in 2014 reports that "while 75 percent of Germans who live in the East said they considered their country's reunification a success, only half of western Germans agreed" (Noack, 2014). Such sentiments are compelling evidence that Germany, decades after reunification, is still divided.

Bibliography

Hartley, E. (2013). "How astronaut Chris Hadfield showed Berlin's ongoing struggle for unification." *The Guardian*, Apr. 21. www.theguardian.com/world/shortcuts/2013/apr/21/astronaut-chris-hadfield-berlin-divide

Noack, R. (2014). "The Berlin Wall fell 25 years ago, but Germany is still divided." *The Washington Post*, October 31. www.washingtonpost.com/news/worldviews/wp/2014/10/31/the-berlin-wall-fell-25-years- ago-but-germany-is-still-divided/?noredirect=on&utm_term=.eb0548ad6cf9

Zeit. (2014). "German Unification: A Nation Divided." ZEIT ONLINE, Nov. 19. Accessed on January 22, 2021. www.zeit.de/feature/german-unification-a-nation-divided

Afterword

Chapter 21: Commentary: Walls Divide
Emily Rodden

Chapter 22: Witnesses of Stone: Monuments of the Socialist Past in Bulgaria
Nikolai Vukov, Ph.D.

CHAPTER 21

Commentary: Walls Divide

Emily Rodden

On 9 November, 1989, the "Iron Curtain that divided Cold War Europe began to develop gaps and holes through which people were able to escape" (Fulbrook, 2011). It was a historic moment, tearing down the division between East and West. The Berlin Wall, built on August 13, 1961 to halt the hemorrhaging of the East German economy, had become the "material symbol of the Cold War division of the world into two moieties within a single city and within a formerly unified territorial state" (Borneman, 1998, p. 157).

Despite its celebrated demise, 30 years after the fall of the Berlin Wall, there is a boom in the building of walls and fortifications around the world. There were seven such structures at the end of WWII, and in 2018, *USA Today* reported that there were at least 77 such barriers today, many erected in the aftermath of the September 11, 2001 terrorist attacks in America.

Walls have been used as barriers for thousands of years. The physical boundary of a wall, in itself, is not problematic. The meaning we attach to walls and what they physically do to separate people is the problem. Walls have been used to support structures, such as buildings; they delineate space; they also serve to construct social borders and define communities. The issue is how we use them, and how people and, often, their governments use them. Walls, particularly those at national borders, serve as barriers to human mobility. It is a way for the nation-state to control territory, and national borders are a key component of state capacity and sovereignty (Zimmer, 2016); as Donnan (1998) points out, it is often

Contributed by Emily Rodden. © Kendall Hunt Publishing Company at the border where state power is most keenly marked and felt. As a physical demarcation between "us" and "them," walls allow for the creation and classification of a foreign "other." Thus, there often emerge many negative consequences, especially regarding human rights, such as the freedom of movement. Arguably, the fortification of borders and the construction of physical barriers harm border communities significantly more than other communities (Zimmer, 2016).

Since the fall of the Berlin Wall in 1989, there has been a resurgence in the construction of massive walls and fortifications. Some for keeping people out, some for keeping people in, and some for different reasons, but nonetheless they are forces of separation and division, dividing the world even more despite globalization's homogenizing impact (Barber, 1991). How do these walls, fences, and barriers affect the people for whom they have intended to keep out (or keep in)?

The discourse of a wall on the southern border of the United States with Mexico arose in the late 1990s when Bill Clinton authorized the construction of a 14-mile-long barrier between San Diego and Tijuana. George W. Bush continued this by signing the Secure Fence Act passed in 2006, enacting the construction of 700 additional miles of fencing on the border (Han & Antrosio, 2019). In the United States, policy makers and the media have intertwined the issues of immigration and terrorism, although they are distinct social processes. As a result, several policies have been proposed and implemented that disproportionately impact communities along the U.S.–Mexico border (Heyman, Morales, & Núñez, 2009). The U.S.–Mexico border is one of the "busiest land borders in the world, the longest and the most dramatic meeting point between a rich and a poor country, and the site of the most intensive interaction between law enforcement and law evasion" (Heyman, 2009). Border communities are calling for a reexamination of the balance between human rights and immigration policing. Such policing creates a new paradigm in Border Patrol efforts, called prevention through deterrence. The effectiveness of this strategy is quite debatable. This paradigm results in a "squeezing of a balloon" effect (Dunn, 2010), which, essentially, displaces immigration from relatively urban, well-trafficked areas, to remote and difficult-to-cross spaces. This makes the immigration process into the United States difficult and even, in some cases, deadly.

We can look at borders like the Berlin Wall as failed attempts to restrict human movement. The Berlin Wall was a representation of a totalitarian government that wanted to exert its power both materially and symbolically through the use of this concrete barrier. The goal was to control goods, ideas, and people, and was frowned upon in much of the international community. Its demise was celebrated all around the world as a remarkable historical event and a representation of the end of an era. Yet today, the United States is now constructing a wall. How are borders affecting people today in the United States, and how should we be addressing them? How is this border perceived on an international level? Knowing how borders affect people, and knowing what borders do to the communities surrounding them, it seems that we should not continue to expand the wall on the U.S.–Mexico border because history will inevitably repeat itself. Borders are made to be torn down.

Bibliography

Barber, B. (1991). Jihad vs. McWorld. *The Atlantic*, Vol. 3 (March).

Borneman, J. (1998). *Subversions of international order: Studies in the political anthropology of culture*. Albany: State University of New York Press.

Dunn, T. (2010). *Blockading the border and human rights: The El Paso Operation that remade immigration enforcement*. Austin: University of Texas Press.

Donnan, H. (1998). Nation, state and identity at international borders. In H. Donnan & TM Wilson (eds.). *Border identities: nation and state at international frontiers* (pp. 1–30). Cambridge: Cambridge University Press.

Han, S., & Antrosio J. (2019). The editors' note: Walls, fences, and barriers: Anthropology on the border. *Open Anthropology* Vol. 7(1):1.

Heyman, J. M., Morales, M. C., & Núñez, G. G. (2009). Engaging with the immigrant human rights movement in a Beseieged border region: What do applied social scientists bring to the policy process? *NAPA Bulletin, 31,* 13–29. doi:10.1111/j.1556-4797.2009.01016.x

Zimmer, K. (2016). "Borders, Fences and Walls: State of Insecurity?" *East/West: Journal of Ukrainian Studies.* DOI: 3.201.10.21226/T2859Z.

CHAPTER 22

Witnesses of Stone: Monuments of the Socialist Past in Bulgaria

Nikolai Vukov, Ph.D.

A visit to almost any town or village in Bulgaria reveals a multitude of monuments, sculptural compositions, and memorial forms dating back to the period of communist rule in this European country. Thirty years after the fall of the Berlin Wall, their omnipresence impresses visitors and locals alike. As elements of the ideological propaganda and its adherent artistic practices after 1944, they reveal the impetus of the communist state to commemorate figures of special importance for the ruling party and to celebrate the new social and political order that was established after World War II. Forming a well-developed memorial landscape, which was propagated as lasting forever, after the end of communist rule some of these monuments and ideological representations were toppled down, substituted or reshaped in new memorial forms—frequently in the midst of public debates and projects for monuments' reinstallation. Although today some of the visual forms of the communist period have left behind only empty pedestals and unrecognisable traces, plenty of memorials and artistic compositions continue to decorate streets and squares—as awkward reminders about one of the most problematic epochs in modern Bulgarian history.

The photo exhibition, *Witnesses of Stone: Monuments of the Socialist Past in Bulgaria*, presents a diversity of photographs of monuments and memorial sites, taken by Luca Ponchiroli, Linda Ferrari & Nikolai Vukov during their field trips around Bulgaria since 2008. The exhibition enables visitors to see dozens of examples of monumental art during communist rule which depict not only the cultural policies and historical representations of that period but also the transformations occurring to these sites of memory after 1989. The exhibition is organized within the framework of the international project, "Heroes We Love: Ideology, Identity and Socialist Art in New Europe," which focused on the controversial topic of the socialist heritage in 20th century European art. The project was supported by the "Creative Europe" Program (2014–2020) and involved participants from several Eastern European countries (Slovenia, Croatia, Bosnia and Herzegovina, Albania, Poland, Serbia, and Bulgaria), which all are undergoing continuing debates on the monumental legacy of the communist period.

Fig. 22.1: *Witnesses of Stone* exhibition in the Francis Harvey Green Library

The exhibition is a visual testimony to the history of monumental art in communist Bulgaria, with references to diverse themes, forms, and representations built between 1944 and 1989. A glance at this history reveals that ideological monuments were raised up almost immediately after the end of World War II. Following the example of the Soviet Union, monument-building was embraced as a state policy and resulted in a multitude of memorial forms that were put in central locations of towns and villages. Parallel to the visual representations of party leaders and prominent personalities of the communist movement, the primary impetus of monument building came with the initiatives to glorify the Soviet army, whose soldiers crossed Bulgarian territory in September 1944. Although war battles did not take place in Bulgaria in the end of World War II, many Soviet soldiers died of their wounds in the country and grand monuments in their honor were raised during the first postwar decade in most of the bigger Bulgarian cities (see Fig. 22.3). In the years that followed, these were complemented by numerous other monuments dedicated to individual Soviet pilots and submariners, or ones with the general purpose of "monuments to the Bulgarian–Soviet friendship."

Parallel to these memorial initiatives, by the first decade after 1944, the communist state developed a widespread practice to commemorate also local examples of war participation. As a result, numerous monuments to the dead in the partisan movement and antifascist resistance started to appear. In the 1960s and 1970s, the building of such monuments was significantly enhanced, covering most of the towns and villages in the country with examples of such memorials. All these were paralleled with a series of monuments to personalities who were special for the regime—starting from Lenin and Marx (see Fig. 22.2), and involving hundreds of communist activists and ideological functionaries (see Figs. 22.4 and 22.5). Another realm of commemorative attention at the time was related to the September 1923 uprising—a social riot, which the regime pronounced as "the first antifascist uprising in the world" and turned into an object of enhanced memorialization. Incorporated firmly into the backbone of communist historiography, it was used as a main reference point in the monuments to the several "revolutionary epochs" and "generations of fighters" that were built in 1960s and 1970s. The latter sought to incorporate the national liberation struggle against the Ottomans in the 19th century with the "socialist revolution" of September 1944, which marked the establishment of the communist rule in the country.

Fig. 22.2: Monument to Lenin in the village of Pet Mogili, Shumen area

Fig. 22.3: Monument to the Soviet army in the town of Russe

Fig. 22.4: Sculptural composition at the base of the "Brotherly Mound to the Fallen in the Antifascist Struggle," Sofia

Fig. 22.5: Monument to fallen antifascists in the village of Hrabrino, Plovdiv area

Fig. 22.6: Sculptural dvecoration representing youth labor and a happy life under communism

A peak in these "sanctifying chronologies" can be seen in the regime's effort to mark the celebration of the 13 centuries after the creation of the Bulgarian State in 1981 by creating panoramas of Bulgarian history in which the communist rule was portrayed as a victorious culmination of centuries of heroic struggle. As part of this effort, in the 1980s a wave of monuments to medieval rulers, educators, and fighters for social justice were built, which provided the regime with the possibility to extend socialist stylistics to historical periods far back into the past. Created by some of the most prominent Bulgarian sculptors and architects at the time, today many of these monuments are viewed as being among the most impressive representations of Bulgarian history, however, also as major examples of communist monumentalism.

Aside from history-related visualizations, a range of other sculptural figures and compositions (of miners, industrial workers, machine laborers, etc.) were also constructed in those years, with the purpose of propagating the glory of the working class and of communist rule as its apotheosis (see Fig. 22.6). No less widely spread were decorations on public buildings and various symbolic compositions (of red stars, flags, hammer and sickle) that animated streets and squares before 1989 (see Fig. 22.7). Although many of them were removed after the fall of the communist regime, such stone representations can still be seen on facades of schools, municipalities, and cultural houses. The ideological "fashion" of creating memorial forms after 1944 is illustrated also in many curious

Fig. 22.7: Interior decoration of the house-monument to the Bulgarian Communist Party on Buzludja Peak

monuments, such as those to tanks, tractors, artillery guns, and airplanes, to workers in different industries, or to participants in the so-called brigadiers' movement, which was organized by the regime in late 1940s for construction work across the country (see Fig. 22.8).

Fig. 22.8: Monument to the first tractor during the postwar mechanization of agriculture, village of Izvorovo, Haskovo area

The exhibition includes photos of monumental structures of all administrative regions in the country and from different places—larger and smaller towns, villages, and district centers. It encompasses diverse artistic and architectural forms: memorials, sculptural compositions, bust monuments, memorial plaques and signs, ideological representations, and compositions with decorative functions. Taken together, they are visual and tangible legacy of the communist period—one that is still present as an immediate reality today and serves as a witness to the memory politics, ideological propaganda, and aesthetics applied by the communist regime. This legacy, which clearly identifies the country as having once belonged to the communist bloc at the eastern side of the Berlin Wall, will continue to attract the wonder and curiosity to country visitors and to the generations of the future.

The Exhibition

Chapter 23: **Making the Exhibition**
Michael A. Di Giovine, Ph.D.

Chapter 24: **Interactive Exhibits in *Faces of the Berlin Wall***
Marshall Goodman and Aiden Max

Chapter 25: **The Art of the West Berlin Wall**
Anissa Kunchick

Chapter 26: **Leaving Our Mark**
Michael A. Di Giovine, Ph.D.

CHAPTER 23

Making the Exhibition

Michael A. Di Giovine, Ph.D.

Faces of the Berlin Wall marks the 11th student co-curated exhibit at West Chester University and the second in the Museum of Anthropology and Archaeology. Sixteen students, equally divided between history majors and anthropology majors, were mentored by expert faculty members as they researched, planned, and executed this ambitious exhibition. Collaboration was key to the success of this exhibition. An early site visit, organized by Dr. Marwan Kredie (Political Science) to visit the German-American Society of Philadelphia—the country's oldest ethnic organization, and one which stewards one of the largest pieces of the Berlin Wall in the United States—led us to our title; students were struck by a mysterious face graffitied onto the cement (look closely at Fig. 25.2, page 203). Colleagues at West Chester University who are experts on Germany, or who had experience in Berlin lent us their artifacts—postcards, photographs, computers, even pieces of the wall that they had collected during that tumultuous and excitement-filled period 30 years ago. In addition, two colleagues in Bulgaria were integral in securing artifacts from the East, and for speaking with the students to adequately contextualize them. Finally, members of our community who hailed from Germany came to speak to our students about their experiences living in the shadow of the Berlin Wall, and I am grateful to them for their generosity in lending their time, their artifacts, and especially their stories. The exhibition was made even richer and more informative because of the generosity of our supportive, extended community.

As with all exhibitions in the museum, which are co-created by students under the auspices of the course, MST 358: Museum Exhibition Curation, students not only learn thematic content germane

Fig. 23.1: Uli Muensch talking with students about his defection from East Germany

to the exhibition—in this case, the history of the Berlin Wall and the Cold War (as they did not live through these modern-day events)—but also practical content on how to mount an exhibition. We discussed and debated the theme: should it be solely about the Berlin Wall, or should be extended to all kinds of walls through history, such as the Great Wall of China or Hadrian's wall? We discussed pedagogy and debated with which message we wanted visitors to leave; this took on particular importance as the United States at the time was mired in discussions over the U.S.–Mexico border wall, border policing, forced internment of migrants, and the intentional separation of migrant families. Espousing different political positions, students were divided—this in and of itself was a productive learning experience! Students saw first-hand the background research necessary for the exhibit—from archival research to oral history elicitation—the fruits of which are in this catalog. Museum designer Tom Haughey, as always, created an ambitious and extraordinary 20-foot-long wall, as well as a scale model of the wall in concrete that weighed at least 500 pounds (even though it is hollow inside), and took several students to move. Students assisted in helping to construct them, and student co-curator Anissa Kunchick worked hard to coordinate the graffitiing of the west side, as well as to etch names of the fallen onto our outdoor model of the wall.

Fig. 23.2: Constructing the wall

Fig. 23.3: Delivering the concrete wall, which would become our memorial to fallen victims

Importantly, the students also experienced the excitement, frustration, and uncertainty that come with mounting a major exhibition (in a quarter of the time a typical exhibition of this size would take). Many of our artifacts were acquisitioned on the museum's behalf by Dr. Rossitza Ohridska-Olson in Sofia, Bulgaria, who kindly Skyped in (before Zooming and Skyping into classes was *de rigueur* in the pandemic age): they included clothing, soaps, toys, tourist souvenirs, books, and many postcards. Unfortunately, the shipment of these artifacts was held up by U.S. customs, and, when it did not appear that we would have what would constitute the bulk of our parallel West Germany-East Germany artifact exhibits, upon which the entire exhibition was largely based, we scrambled to revise and reorganize the exhibition. Fortunately, the boxes arrived just two days before the exhibition opening, and the

Fig. 23.4: Cataloging artifacts from Eastern Europe

students worked tirelessly to study, catalog, and exhibit the artifacts. They did a superb job!

Finally, coinciding with the opening of *Faces of the Berlin Wall*, our colleagues in Bulgaria also mounted two associated exhibitions on the side. These were both featured in the Francis Harvey Green Library. Dr. Nikolai Vukov, who came to West Chester University from his post at the Museum of Ethnology in Sofia to serve as a consultant for the opening of the exhibition, mounted *Witnesses in Stone*, a photo essay about Soviet-era monuments' second life as heritage in Bulgaria; he also presented a public lecture here and at Bloomsburg University in association with the exhibition (see Chapter 22). In addition, Dr. Ohridska-Olson worked (via Skype) with student co-curators Shahd El Gerzawy and Aaron Gallant to mount an aesthetically and intellectually compelling exhibition, *Postcard Memories*, on the role of postcards in creating a shared geographic and cultural identity among those living in the Eastern bloc (see Chapter 9).

Fig. 23.5: 8th and 9th graders from Unionville High School tour the exhibition with co-curators Christian Sabree (left) and Aaron Gallant (right)

With a number of positive reviews in area newspapers and magazines, we were fortunate to have utilized this exhibition for a range of community programming, and hosted several middle school and high school groups—public and private schools, as well as home-schooled groups—; teen centers such as Kennett Square's Garage Youth Center, and senior groups coming from as far as Wilmington, Delaware—in addition to hundreds of West Chester University students. Our co-curators eagerly presented their exhibits to the groups. The Center for International Programs found the exhibition particularly useful in engaging their international exchange students and those in English as a foreign language groups. Many classes also visited, and we are grateful for Dr. Brenda Gaydosh's graduate history class who—inspired by the exhibition—contributed short pieces to this catalog as well (see Chapters 5, 7, 10, and 19). Finally, an area high school student, Senthil Vel, came to our class meetings several times to document the process and interview several of the student co-curators for a senior project. His video is featured on our website, and several of his photos appear in this book.

Fig. 23.6: Deconstructing the wall

Arguably, the exhibition on the fall of the Berlin Wall would not be complete without a ceremonial "tearing down" of the wall. This occurred a year later, one week before the university museum would unexpectedly close because of the pandemic. Several of the student co-curators had already graduated. Nevertheless, a new group of co-curators, already working on planning the following exhibition celebrating the 50th anniversary of Earth Day, helped. We carefully preserved the interactive graffiti portion of the wall, which is presented at the end of Chapter 26 in this catalog. De-installing an exhibition is always a little sad, a little nostalgic; but the inclusion of this new group of eager co-curators makes it an especially hopeful time as we turn our sights on hosting another extraordinary exhibition.

CHAPTER 24

Interactive Exhibits in *Faces of the Berlin Wall*

Marshall Goodman and Aiden Max

Faces of the Berlin Wall commemorates the 30th anniversary of the fall of the Berlin Wall. The central message is the Berlin Wall was not just a wall, but a culmination of lived experiences that has had a global cultural impact and continues to be relevant 30 years later. This exhibit is broken into multiple sections, each worked on by a different group of students. By dividing these sections into two sides, it creates its own constructivist learning opportunity by allowing members to choose where they wish to go. This method of presentation, in itself, is interactive and educational (Bedford, 2014, p. 34). But within the exhibition, there are three areas in which interaction was a primary consideration. These are the interactive Apple iPad 2, the graffiti wall, and the touchable scale model-cum-memorial outside the museum.

The interactive Apple iPad 2 brings together the entire Daily Life portion of the main exhibit into one condensed space and it also allows for hands-on learning to create a more immersive experience for visitors. The device enables a hands-on learning experience for visitors, where the focus is on the visitor and their needs, rather than on the artifacts themselves (Hein, 1995, p. 78). In addition, the interactive opens up the opportunity for people to explore more information not included in the exhibit labels if they desire to do so. The intention of adding the Apple iPad 2 is to be user-friendly, and not to just be some unexplorable bank of information (Caulton,

Contributed by Marshall Goodman and Aiden Max.
© Kendall Hunt Publishing Company

Fig. 24.1: Tablet home page

1998, p. 24). Not only does it have information on some of the objects in the Daily Life portion of the exhibit, but it also includes interviewed stories of some of those involved, and videos showing events that people experienced.

The tablet allows guests to have more interaction with the exhibit itself and aids those interested in obtaining more knowledge on daily life in Berlin. When navigating the accompanying website, the visitor is presented with two options: West Berlin and East Berlin; following the layout design of the main exhibit where a visitor must pick which side to travel, they also have to make the same decision with the website. When the visitor selects the West Berlin option, for example, they will be taken to a new page that will offer more information on objects, stories, and videos. Reflecting the color scheme of the exhibition, pages corresponding to West Berlin have a yellow theme. However, it was decided not to include *all* of the artifacts in the website because while our goal was to offer more information, we did not want to clutter the website. At the bottom of the artifacts page, there is the option "Tap here to compare objects to the ones on the East side." Tapping this takes the visitor to the East Objects page, and vice-versa.

Likewise, the "Stories" menu presents the oral histories of the four people included in the "Through Their Eyes" exhibit, Kordula Segler-Stahl and Barbara Raichel Soringer on the West side, and Ivonne Finnin (Nitsche) and Ulirich Meunch on the East side. Each is given their own page, in which their story and an optional audio recording (where applicable) is available. Finally, if the visitor chooses the "Videos" option, they are offered a variety of videos showing the lived experiences of the respective sides of the wall. The visitor can select and watch the video of their choice.

There are also two other interactives available for visitors, ones that encourage tactile interactions, albeit in a technologically simpler fashion. The wall itself has a section free of graffiti on which visitors are encouraged to leave their mark. Our intention is to provide them the opportunity to express themselves in a similar manner to those in West Germany. We encourage visitors to graffiti this portion of the wall because it allows them to experience for themselves the creative act of rebellion that West Germans felt. While the museum context is, of course, quite different from the lived experiences of the wall during the Cold War, tagging public space—especially in a museum setting and university building—is quite taboo; and as Duncan (1995) argues, museums typically were employed to "civilize" and instruct their visitors in proper social action. Participating in this action, after learning about the graffiti on the Berlin Wall, also serves to generate an iterative and deeply personal impression, which

Fig. 24.2: WCU students in the ELS program leave their mark on the wall

Fig. 24.3: Museum Director Michael A. Di Giovine's children graffiting the wall

will shape and reinforce visitors knowledge of the topic (Bedford, 2014, p. 33). We found people generally have a greater connection to something if they can interact with it physically, and allowing viewers to write a message or draw something on the wall provides a unique experience that separates our exhibit from other Berlin Wall exhibitions around the world. Consequently, this is clearly the most popular portion of the exhibition, especially with middle- and high-school students.

Outside the Museum of Anthropology and Archaeology, we installed a scale model of a section of the Berlin Wall itself. This structure provides a chance to physically touch the barrier, providing a greater, more embodied understanding of the wall. Like the original sections of the Berlin Wall, this miniature version was made of poured concrete and rebar, with a cantilevered bottom. The front of the wall, which would have faced westward, is graffitied while the back is left in bare concrete. On top of the graffiti are some of the names of the 196 Germans who died trying to cross the border—a lasting memorial that once again humanizes the concrete structure.

Museum studies have emphasized the physical urge of visitors to touch installations and monuments and objects that are closely associated with the human body (Di Giovine, 2009), and contemporary monuments such as Maya Lin's Vietnam Veterans Memorial has harnessed this to great success (Smith, 2000). Indeed, our own memorial, which has weathered over time, has become itself a spot for visitors to gaze at and photograph; it has also elicited questions about its authenticity as a real piece of the wall!

By incorporating these hands-on, tactile, and interactive components, the exhibition can cater to a broad museum public (Caulton, 1998, p. 28). Constructivist in nature, it offers visitors the ability to construct their own knowledge and understanding of the exhibit through personal and social interaction. This creates, we hope, what Kuh (2008) calls a "high impact education practice"—one that will help successfully convey information that will remain with the visitor long after the exhibition is complete.

Fig. 24.4: Anissa Kunchick painting the memorial to fallen victims

Fig. 24.5: Ivonne Finnin examining the memorial

Bibliography

Bedford, L. (2014). *The art of museum exhibitions: How story and imagination create aesthetic experience.* Walnut Creek, CA: Left Coast Press.

Caulton, T. (1998). *Hands-on exhibitions: Managing interactive museums and science centres.* London: Routledge.

Di Giovine, M. (2009). Body worlds and body world 2: Towards the creation of an instructive museum of man. *Museum Anthropology Review, 3*(1). Accessed on February 7, 2021 from https://scholarworks.iu.edu/journals/index.php/mar/article/view/104.

Duncan, C. (1995). *Civilizing rituals.* London: Routledge.

Hein, G. (1995). *The constructivist museum*. London and New York: Routledge.

Kuh, G. (2008). *High-impact educational practices*. Washington, DC: Association of American Colleges and Universities.

Smith, L. (2000). Window or mirror: The Vietnam veterans memorial and the ambiguity of remembrance. In Peter Homans (ed.). *Symbolic loss* (pp. 105–125). Charlottesville, VA: University Press of Virginia.

CHAPTER 25

The Art of the West Berlin Wall

Anissa Kunchick

The abstract and vibrant graffiti on the west side of the Berlin Wall is without a doubt the most picturesque message it has to offer. With its creative, political, and sometimes grotesque narrative, this rebellious act of artistic expression embodied what the wall had to offer the world—freedom, love, hate, anger, remorse, and hope (see Hohensee, n.d.). Graffiti upon the wall would be a permanent mark on a temporary world, and thus became the chosen method of many West Berliners to leave a lasting impact. Pictured below (Fig. 25.1) are references recreated onto our own Berlin Wall, which includes not only anonymous faces and tags—such as an alligator and other images captured by photographer Tamás Urbán (Rian, 2017)—but also several iconic images painted after the fall in the East Side Gallery, such as Thierry Noir's *Cartoon Heads* and Margaret Hunter's *Joint Venture*. Our student artists also improvised as well, leaving our own mark in this exhibit.

In addition, our initial class visit to the German Society of Philadelphia allowed us to look at a piece of the wall up-close, inspecting the graffitied west side and a rather blank east side (Fig. 25.2). We were particularly struck by an anonymous image of a face—this provided us with the title of the exhibition, *Faces of the Berlin Wall*. In researching the art of the Berlin Wall (see, for example, Dundon 2017; Jones 2014; Moscatello 2014), I was struck by the work of Margaret Hunter, a British artist who was invited to paint similar faces on the east side of the wall in 1990 in a work she called "Joint Venture" (Hunter n.d.;

220 CHAPTER 25 The Art of the West Berlin Wall

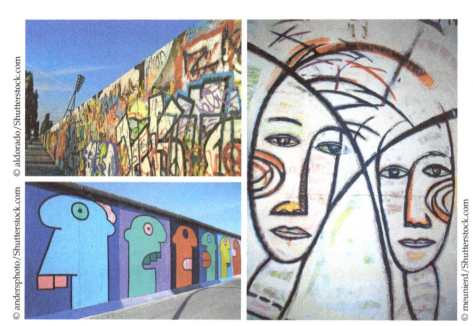

Fig. 25.1: Images from Berlin Wall graffiti that provided inspiration for our interpretation. Top left: View of the western side of the wall; Thierry Noir's *Cartoon Heads*; Margaret Hunter's *Joint Venture*.

see Fig. 25.1, right). The ideas of dual faces, as well as being able to create graffiti upon a blank concrete canvas—portraying unification and division—resonated with our exhibition theme.

The graffiti were not the only artistic flourishes placed in this exhibit. As with most museum galleries, we have provided exhibition visitors places to sit and enjoy the art. Flanking both sides of the wall, exhibits designer Thomas Haughey has created replica Bauhaus benches. Although the Bauhaus movement predated the Cold War, this year also marks the 100th anniversary of the foundation of this artistic movement. We included the following label:

> The gray benches and chairs you might be sitting on were constructed in the Bauhaus style, an incredibly influential modernist artistic movement in 20th century Germany. Celebrating its 100th anniversary this year, Bauhaus was founded by Walter Gropius in Weimar, in what would become East Germany in 1919, shortly after WWI. An architect by trade, Gropius envisioned this art movement as

Fig. 25.2: Graffiti of a mysterious face on the German Society of Philadelphia's Berlin Wall segment.

creating a *Gesamtkunstwerk* ("total work of art") in which all arts, including architecture, crafts, and visual arts would be brought together. He later opened its school in Berlin, where it was active until the Nazi regime; Hitler outlawed it as "degenerate art" and persecuted its purveyors. Nevertheless, it had a profound influenced on graphic design, art, architecture, and industrial design, and influenced such greats as Mies van der Rohe.

Fig. 25.3: Student co-curator Christian Sabree enjoys a minute of calm before the Opening Reception

All of this art served as an inspiration, and point of departure, for our *bricolage* version of the west side of the Berlin Wall (Fig. 25.4).

Fig. 25.4: Side view of Bauhaus benches and west side of the wall

Bibliography

Dundon, R. (2017). This photographer's collection of Berlin Wall graffiti photos show the politics of paint. *Timeline*. Oct. 27. Accessed on January 24, 2021. https://timeline.com/berlin-wall-photos-graffiti-bc62b7cccf62

Hohensee, N. (n.d.). The Berlin Wall as political symbol. *Khan Academy*. Accessed on January 24, 2021. https://www.khanacademy.org/humanities/art-1010/architecture-design/late-modernismpost-modernism/a/the-berlin-wall-as-a-political-symbol-edit

Hunter, M. (n.d.) *Joint Venture* and *Re-Statement*. Accessed on January 24, 2021. http://www.margaret-hunter.com/joint_venture_restatement.html

Jones, J. (2014). Thierry Noir: The first graffiti artist fired up by the Berlin Wall. *The Guardian,* April 3. Accessed on January 24, 2021. https://www.theguardian.com/artanddesign/jonathanjonesblog/2014/apr/03/thierry-noir-graffiti-artist-berlin-wall

Moscatello, C. (2014). The art of the Berlin Wall: A tale of two cities. Condé Nast Traveler. November 7. Accessed on January 24, 2021. https://www.cntraveler.com/galleries/2014-11-07/the-art-of-the-berlin-wall-a-tale-of-two-cities

CHAPTER 26

Leaving Our Mark

Michael A. Di Giovine, Ph.D.

Arguably the most popular aspect of *Faces of the Berlin Wall* was the opportunity for visitors to contribute their own graffiti in a specially designated interactive space on our wall. Our student co-curators recognized visitors' desire to viscerally share in the imaginaries of that period of youthful rebellion and political protest (and also were concerned that, if there were no designated place, people would write everywhere!). It was a hit.

"I LOVED the Berlin Wall. It was so cool how we got to sign our names on the wall," wrote Evie, an eighth-grade student, in a thank you letter after a visit with student co-curators (see Fig. 26.1). "Thank you for letting us do graffiti," echoed Timothy. Yet another wrote, "It's amazing how the Stasi kept one side from touching the wall and let the other side write all over it," subtly revealing the pedagogical lesson we sought to convey. Our interactive graffiti wall was meant to engage visitors, body and mind, fostering self-reflexivity: "I calculated and my mom would have been twenty when they took down the wall," another student wrote, making connections with her own life.

Middle schoolers from the West Chester community were not the only ones to graffiti the wall; so, too, did students, faculty, and staff. There were no instructions, except to "leave your own graffiti here," yet the markings left closely paralleled themes from the original wall, but with a 21st century twist. Personal markings included names of lovers, but also exhortations to follow the writers on their social media handles. Beautiful pictures were drawn (sometimes in response to someone else's earlier tag), as were silly or banal phrases, or pop cultural references. And political messages were

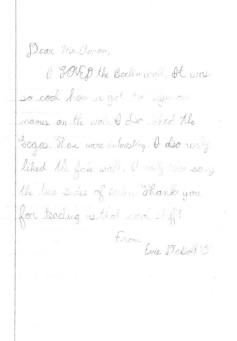

Fig. 26.1: Letter from an 8th-grade student

scrawled—many of them directly speaking to the lessons learned in this exhibit: "Walls don't work" or "Tear down the wall" could be read. In some cases, political arguments were carried over time, with responses and counter-responses written.

A month after the opening, when there was already a significant amount of graffiti, I spied one of our student co-curators walking to the wall with a can of gray touch-up paint. "What are you doing with that?" I asked. "I'm just covering up some inappropriate comments," he said innocently. At first, I assumed he was painting over something risqué—akin to what one might find in a public men's room stall—but it turned out that this was not the case (and in fact, there was never any graffiti like that on our wall; Carol Duncan's (1995) argument that museums are "civilizing institutions" that enculturate visitors toward behaving in a certain way may just be true!). Rather, he was worried about pro-border wall political messaging that someone had written, likely in response to the exhibit. This was, after all, the height of the Trump administration's contested border wall policy, which sought to deter undocumented migrants through increased militarization of the border, the intentional separation of families, and the construction of a "big, beautiful" wall. I stopped the student. No, this should be treated as a living document, a space where visitors can feel comfortable communicating with each other. As an anthropology major, he could even treat it like "data"—a written time capsule for posterity, providing insight into the issues—serious and banal—that occupy our visitors' hearts, minds, and energy.

And so it grew. Our little slice of the wall quickly filled up, and visitors searched for new places, high and low; along the corners and on the narrow sides. They took chairs to reach higher up the 15-foot-high wall; some, like the students in the picture below (Fig. 26.2) even climbed on each other. Like the "real" wall, it left an intriguing documentation of a particular time and place.

Fig. 26.2: Students from Windsor Academy creatively find blank space to graffiti the wall.

Figs. 26.3a, b, c, d: Samples of visitors' graffiti

When the exhibition came to an end and it came time to de-install, the museum had to "tear down that wall"—in the famous words of Ronald Reagan. While we needed to repurpose the beautifully decorated wall, we saved the interactive graffiti portion of it for posterity. Perhaps in the decades to come, a new generation of young anthropologists will mine it for insights.

Bibliography

Duncan, C. (1995). *Civilizing rituals*. London: Routledge.